home is always

the place you just left

A MEMOIR OF RESTLESS LONGING
AND PERSISTENT GRACE

betty smartt carter

PARACLETE PRESS

BREWSTER, MASSACHUSETTS

Scripture quotations are taken from the King James Bible.

Library of Congress Cataloging-in-Publication Data
Smartt Carter, Betty, 1965–
Home is always the place you just left : a memoir of restless longing
and persistent grace / by Betty Smartt Carter.
      p. c.m.
Includes bibliographical references.
     ISBN 1-55725-323-4 (pbk.)
1. Smartt Carter, Betty, 1965- 2. Presbyterians—United States—
Biography. I. Title.
BX9225.S474 A3 2003
285'.1'092— dc21   2003000167

10 9 8 7 6 5 4 3 2 1

Published by Paraclete Press
Brewster, Massachusetts
www.paracletepress.com
Printed in the United States of America.

To *Julie Sparkman, my teacher*

contents

Introduction

This is a story about how God revealed himself to me before I knew I was looking for him. I now see that God is always revealing himself to us: through family, through friends, through beauty, and, ultimately, through suffering. These are signs on the road, pointing us straight to the door of heaven. The door looks a little different to everybody, but that doesn't matter. By the time we get there, we don't care about anything but stepping through it.

I first learned about God in my relationship with my mother. She taught me the two most important points of theology: that God loves us and that he's good. As a five-year-old, I wanted to be crucified with Jesus, and once tried to do the job myself. Later I scratched Bible verses on sidewalks with chalk and declared I'd grow up to be a missionary. You'd think, given such a great head start, that I'd have found God early on: I'd have been glowing with spiritual fulfillment at least by junior high school. But the journey proved to be long and difficult. It's not finished yet, and I still resist it.

John Donne wrote in his *Holy Sonnets*,

> *Batter my heart, three-personed God . . .*
> *That I may rise and stand, o'erthrow me, and bend*
> *Your force to break, blow, burn, and make me new. . . .**

What is it like to be overthrown in order to rise and stand? How does it feel to be bent, broken, blown, burned, and made new? It feels like hell. God's battering is not easy; his burning is not quick. Many a day, I'd have preferred a nice aneurysm. And though now I see that the results of God's burning are good, I won't lie and say I'd do it all over again.

I don't know why God makes us go through suffering when he could heal us with a word. I don't know why we have to suffer the agonies, the indignities of this temporal life. I haven't figured it out yet, though I've heard plenty of theories, and met plenty of people ready to expatiate on the subject. Maybe the best I can do is consider what the question itself means, and then look to the cross, where Jesus himself cried out "Why?"

> *My God, my God, why hast thou forsaken me?***

Those words are Christ's gift to all of us who've wondered whether suffering has any point. They offer no answer to the mystery of pain, only kinship in grief, and a rebuke to any human being who claims to understand why a loving God asks his children to endure hardship.

At times over the years, I've ached for the easy belief of my childhood. I thought I could deal with unhappiness if I could also have joy and passion. I wanted miracles. No such luck, since I was Presbyterian. I longed for beauty and mystery, and I'd given up hope of finding either in the tradition that formed me. Then when I warmed to God, I found the mystery and beauty of the gospel itself, which transcends but also inhabits all Christian traditions. For believers, the gospel of Jesus *is* beauty: beauty written into story. The cross is our treasure. It's our flame in the bush. It's the hot blood flowing through the veins of the Bride of Christ, yes even through her Presbyterian appendages.

I confess, I still feel much shame when I look back at the past. It gives me no joy to recall how low I've sunk. Certainly it gives me no joy to reveal this sinkage before the world. I'd rather hold on to a little dignity, pretending to myself, to God, that I'm a naturally buoyant creature, that I've always kept my head above water, and these days barely sink at all.

But what's the good of dignity if it's only a show? I remember that a few years ago I went to a little circus here in my hometown and saw a woman perform with trained poodles. The poodles danced in hoop skirts. One was dressed up like Scarlett O'Hara in the Atlanta jail scene: all in green velvet, with lots of fringe and little pompoms tied under a furry chin. It teetered daintily on nervous hind paws, trying not to trip over its voluminous dress. Meanwhile a man walked around behind it with a shovel and scooped elephant poop off the concrete floor of the Leeds National Guard Armory.

Suddenly, I identified with the poodle. I sat there with my two nice kids, looking respectable enough, but knowing I was just a dog in a hoop skirt. I figured the poodle must hate the circus like I hated my life. I felt the most acute shame.

I've been freed from the worst of that shame, thank God, but I still see life as more or less a poodle show. Human existence is comedy within tragedy within comedy. Even at our very glorious human best—when we sing holy songs, write poetry, tell stories—we possess only a measure of glory. Our flesh is an old coat of fur that we cover up as best we can. But there's really no shame in that at all. God loves us. One day he'll give us new bodies, without the suffering and the sadness that cling to our old ones like grime. Until then, we should keep singing, keep writing poems, keep telling our stories—especially the stories of God's grace to us. This is mine.

1

The Smarrts, circa 1968
Left to right: Danny, Mary, Kennedy, Betty, Matthew, and Ellen

night terrors,
button jars

Lord, how long wilt thou look on?
Rescue my soul from their destructions,
my darling from the lions.

—Psalm 35:17

I don't know why I had to discover God in the particular way I did, through suffering. "Why" is a funny question, anyway. When things are bad, people go around asking it ad nauseam.

"Why can't I be rich?"

"Why won't he love me?"

"Why did I have to get sick?"

Everybody I know asks why. But a friend from India once told me that the question isn't universal: it pops up only in western societies, where reason and science have crowded out mystery. He said that Hindus, for example, don't naturally expect to find causes behind natural events. My flipping a switch in New Delhi doesn't make the light appear in the bulb, even if the switch has a large sign hanging from it that says "Flip here to turn on light." He told me all this at a party where he wouldn't stop pretending to be an elderly secretary named Beatrice, until my husband nearly strangled him and threw him out the door. Under those circumstances, it was hard not to discount everything he said. I argued that even devout and mystically minded Hindus must sometimes ask why:

"Why does my wife always smile at the dentist?"

"Why is that dog wearing a sweater?"

"Why did you put a scorpion in my pajamas?"

 Small questions lead to great ones:

"Why do good people do evil deeds?"

"Why in this beautiful world should there be so much suffering?"

Actually, "Why?" may be the most devout question any human being can ask, because of what it implies about God. If I ask, "How did the universe get here?" I'm showing curiosity. If I ask, "Who made all this?" I'm only admitting that some powerful being may be necessary to explain so much matter and energy swirling around in nothingness, like dirty footprints on a kitchen floor. But if I ask, "*Why* is the universe here?" or even "*Why* do I get canker sores after eating strawberries?" I show that I hope for order in this mess. I want to know whether God tramps through nothingness for a reason, and whether all this junk, this frenzied mud I wade through from one second to the next, is maybe a trail that leads somewhere. To ask why shows that I have expectations, and expectations are the beginning of faith—however small, however many times crushed and reborn.

Somewhere along the way, I stopped having expectations. Even in the worst of my adult unhappiness, it didn't occur to me to ask "Why am I alive?" or "Why do things have to be like this?" To remember faith—to remember how to ask why—I must return to an April morning in 1965, when I enter the world as we know it. A circle of church women welcomes me with Jello-mold hairdos and pale cotton dresses. Their warm Virginia voices surround my mother's shoulders. They shower her with gifts for "the late baby." A few weeks later, I kick my fat feet in the air, a sock flutters down like a fuzzy bird, and a warm, wet hand settles over my matted hair. A voice says, "I baptize you in the name of the Father, and of the Son, and of the Holy Ghost." I squint at my earthly father, who smiles at me from several feet away against a backdrop of chandeliers and balcony rail, and then at my mother, who glances nervously at my brothers and sister on the front pew to see whether they're behaving themselves. I leave the hands of the guest preacher who has just baptized me and is probably wondering whether my mother will have roast beef or chicken for dinner after Sunday school.

Looking like a drowned cat, I go forth into the loving arms of my parents and the congregation. I am now *in*—a bona fide member of the Covenant Family, Southern Presbyterian branch. The next step will be to make it through my toddler years and then learn the Westminster Shorter Catechism, watered down for late-twentieth-century preschoolers.

"Who made you?"

"God."

"What else did God make?"

"All things."

"*Why* did God make you and all things?"

"For his own glory."

A few years after my baptism, my mother teaches me these first few questions from the Children's Catechism. I don't remember the exact evening, but I see that she kneels with a yellow booklet tilted back against her chest. She's around forty-three. The cultural revolution of the 1960s is in full swing, and fashions have begun to swing, too, even for pastors' wives. Her lipstick is pale purple and shines on her lower lip like new paint on a windowsill. Her knees show under her dress. She still has her hair permed each month (by Miss Helen Price), but the style is smooth and loose. Her eyes are blue and large. She has a strong nose: sometimes I pull it to make sure she's really Mama. (Mr. Harshbarger next door has told me a story about an alligator that disguised itself as a certain woman and stole into her house to eat her children. The way you check to see if your mother is really an alligator is by yanking on her nose, which I do, as often as the story comes to mind.)

I have a music box by my bed with a ballerina that stands up and pirouettes when you turn a key underneath. Lying there, I turn the key almost to the stripping point, and then Mama and I watch the ballerina for a couple of quiet minutes, admiring the glow of yellow light from the lamp on the bedstand.

"Betty," she says, returning to our catechism questions, "*Why* did God make you and all things?"

"For his own glory."

"That's right. And how ought you to glorify God?"

"By loving him and doing what he commands."

"Yes, that's right. By loving him and doing what he commands." About now, Mama may be thinking how God created me for his own glory when she hadn't meant to create me at all. Three children had always seemed like plenty to her. But I came along by accident, and this only confirmed to her that God made me for a special purpose, apart from any plans of her own. Not that she's all that Presbyterian in her theology: she complains to herself (if not to Daddy) that our kind of Presbyterianism is too intellectual. She misses a particular camp in New York State. It's the place where she found Jesus, and up there the Holy Spirit was so present that you could almost see him moving through the chapel at night, when people gathered to pray. At that camp, they talked about the Christian life as constant warfare against the devil, which is exactly how Mama sees it. She's on the lookout for Satan. She knows that to love God and do what he commands means to endure afflictions from the Prince of the Power of the Air: suffering and catastrophe such as one can only bear with the help of the Spirit. She's already borne some of it herself, with the death of her dearest brother (when he was eighteen) and then her father, several years ago.

About now I'm certainly not considering why God made me. That seems so obvious since I, tiny and pale and lying under my soft sheets in my cotton nightgown, am absolutely necessary to the flow of the universe. My mother revolves around me like the sun around the earth, casting her golden glow. God is far above us both, watching, and of course we're here because if we weren't, why should anything else be here, either? We are essential. We are (together, not separately) both the event and the cause for the event. Why should the ballerina dance in the box? Why should a train whistle blow behind the trees outside my window? Only for us.

What I am considering is whether this pretty woman who seems to be my mother might really be an alligator (even though I've now checked a couple of times), or whether a bony, bloody hand might poke up through my mattress once she's left the room—I'm always worrying that there's a hand in my bed. If it's there, I figure it must be the hand of Satan himself, a claw of that same devil my mother's always looking out for when catastrophes befall us.

I interrupt the catechism to ask for a clarification. "Isn't it kind of proud for God to want people to glorify him all the time?"

Mama looks a little taken aback.

"It's bad to be proud, right? You said pride is a sin."

"Oh no," she answers in a gentle, shocked voice. "Pride isn't a sin for God. It's all right for God to want glory because he really deserves it. He's eternal. He never makes mistakes and he never changes. He has no beginning and no end."

I try to imagine what it means to have no beginning, and I can't. The thought frightens me. I don't want the world or even time itself to be much bigger than my own house. I like the idea, though, that God will never change. I picture him as an enormous, white mass circling the earth like a glacier, holding it all intact.

We pray, "Now I lay me down to sleep, I pray the Lord my soul to keep. If I should die before I wake, I pray the Lord my soul to take." Then my mother kisses me and before she goes, we argue about which of us loves the other one more.

"I love you a bushel and a peck," she says.

"Well," I say, stretching out my stick arms, "I love you a thousand bushels and a thousand hundred million pecks."

And that's supposed to be the end of conversation for the day. She pulls the door slowly to, leaving a thin crack, and cuts off the light so that the room changes utterly. I don't really mind the dark until she's gone from the doorway, out of sight, like the sun going over the edge of the world. Then I'm alone in this black place with a tiny tickle in my spine, the tip of a knotty finger.

My heart begins to race. My eyes open as wide as saucers. The black of the room turns to orange-gray, like crumbled ash. A warm wind swirls in the windows and curtain shadows leap up the wall. I roll to the very edge of the bed, trying to escape from the bump in the middle, but now I remember that there are demons, right down there on the floor! Every evening they coil up like snakes in the tumbleweed dust, waiting. Then when the light goes off, they slither out from under my bed, looking for tiny feet. I couldn't possibly put my feet down, not on that floor, not for anything, not for a million dollars. But I want to. The truth is, I can hardly help myself! I might do it! Oh, please Jesus, help me not to get out of this bed!

"Mama!" I yell. "Mama, come here!"

A few seconds pass and then she glides in, leaving the door open wide, and smiling sweetly. Her face is bright, even in the shadows. She already knows why I've called.

"Yes?"

"Mama, I'm afraid of the dark."

"Oh dear." She sighs and kneels by my bed to pray with me again. "Lord, help Betty to trust in you. Help her to know that you're always with her, watching over her, that you see everything, that you're more powerful than any of her fears. . . ." She keeps talking for a while, until I lose track of the words and forget to close my eyes. On "Amen" I snap them shut again, quickly.

"You'll be all right now," she says. I open my eyes. She stays for a minute, kisses me, and then leaves.

I wait a while to see if the prayer took. I wait a good five minutes or even ten minutes. In the living room, two walls away, the rest of my family sits down to watch television, everybody except my invalid grandmother, who's also been put to bed early. Even with my door almost shut, I can hear the tinny applause from the old black-and-white television. My father and mother and brothers and sister suddenly burst into warm laughter. Oh, how can they be so heartless, making all that happy noise while I lie in here alone?

Suddenly something crashes in the closet by my bed. So! The prayer didn't take!

"Mama!" I yell. "Mama!" I keep yelling until she shows up at the door again with her hands on her hips.

"Yes, sweetheart? Did you call me?"

"There's something in my room."

"No, sweetheart, there's not."

"I hear something. Look in the closet."

She walks past my sister's bed and opens the door in the corner. "No, there's nothing in here. It's all clear."

"Could you pray for me again?"

She takes a deep breath. "When we trust in Jesus, we have nothing to fear. Repeat to yourself 'Perfect love casts out fear.'"

I think that's easy for her to say, since she's out there watching *The Price is Right* while Satan himself bangs around in my closet. But she's said what she could, and that's all she's going to say for now and I know it. She leaves again, and I'm alone.

The third time I call her she appears after a minute, thrusts open the door quickly, and says, "Now, you must go to sleep!"

"But I can't."

"Obey Mama. Go to sleep."

"Why?"

"Because it's bedtime and little girls need sleep."

"Why?"

"Because I said so."

"But *why?*" I ask in my most logical voice, as if I really care about the reason.

"Because I said so."

I start to cry. "Why can't I sleep in your bed? There's plenty of room in your bed."

"You must not call me again."

Oh, actually, I must. A fourth and then a fifth time. Around the sixth or seventh call, my father enters the room like Zeus on a thundercloud, and I don't call my mother anymore because if I do I'm sure to have the devil spanked out of me right here, right now. No more pleading tonight. I lie in the dark asking God to take away all the bad things and protect me from evil spirits. An hour later, my ten-year-old sister comes to sleep in the bed next to mine, bringing a little peace. She tells me a story to help me sleep. She lets me roll up at the foot of her bed, wrapped in the end of her spread.

But in the middle of the night I wake up and it starts again. I have to pee! I try to hold it, but I can't. I don't want to wet the bed. So while everyone else is sleeping, I put one foot on the floor, and I'm sure I'm about to feel cold demon fingers around my ankle. I wait. No fingers. I put the other foot down. Still no demons. But as I walk the long, black mile to the bathroom, I hear a voice. . . .

"Betty. Betty."

I stop, because a voice is calling me in the darkness. It's a woman's voice, floating down from above my head. No, it's not my mother's voice, or my sister's or even my grand-mother's, but it sounds gentle enough and friendly. I don't feel a bit afraid. So I turn, expecting to see a face, and I see nothing but blackness. I am all alone in the hall. Completely alone.

I know I shouldn't call my mother again! But I push myself forward, down the hall toward Mama and Daddy's bedroom, still trying not to wet my nightgown. Every step is an effort. I feel my way along the smooth paint of the wall, running my hands over a picture frame. The hall is so long and wide.

"Betty," calls the voice again.

I gather all my breath. "Mama!" I yell in a voice loud enough to wake up the whole house. "Mama, I want you!"

My cry hangs in the air for a moment, and then suddenly I see the most joyful sight. A warm band of light flicks on under my parents' door. Suddenly, I have the strength to whirl around and thump back to my room, panting. I leap over the end board, onto my pillow, and slide into the sheets.

A few seconds pass. There are stirring noises down the hall. I wait, grateful to be here, but also pretty sure it will be my father who comes, paddle in hand, scary as a nightmare. Then the door opens and . . . miraculous to tell! My mother strides into the room in her thin pink gown, pressing the curlers deeper into her hair. Her eyes are sleepy, but at least she's here. She climbs into my bed, pats me, and lies down with her back against mine, not saying a word. I sigh a deep sigh. The golden light shines again. Darkness has fled. I finally go to sleep again, not to wake till morning.

When morning comes, she's gone. I walk down the hall and into her room, where she sits in her flower-print chair reading her Bible, as she does every morning. I crawl up in her lap and run my finger down the thin paper on the page. She gets out her jar of buttons. I try to match them on her bed—thin disks of blue and pink and black and gold and silver, some covered in satin, some stamped with anchors, daisies, or ribbons. I imagine all the dresses and coats and blouses my mother wore in those unimaginable years before I was born, in those days when I hadn't even been thought of yet. I'm glad my mother came first: I'm glad she's stronger than I— strong enough to protect me in the middle of the night.

Scripture says that perfect love casts out fear. Mama's love may fall short of perfect, but when she's with me, I fear nothing. This is the closest place to heaven I know, and later in life, I'll long to come here again, back to this house and to these almost perfect moments. I will look for this comfort everywhere, and I'll find it nowhere, until the search itself begins to torment me worse than a bony hand in a box spring, a floorful of demons, a hall of ghostly voices. But the search will also bring God down that hall—mighty but gentle, scattering my evil visions and bringing peace.

And what about the voice? My adult self wants to know what actually happened that night on the way to the bathroom. I take the rational and perhaps Western approach: I observe a result (voices and visions, waking dreams) and search for a likely cause (a sleep disorder? latent schizophrenia?). I think that maybe the voice I heard was only static in my child's brain: echoes from dreams and night terrors. Actual demons sound unlikely (since when have they bothered about Presbyterians?). On the other hand, maybe an evil spirit *did* make the hair stand up on my neck that night. Even a supernatural cause is a cause, and to uncover a cause always brings enlightenment.

As a child in the hall, I knew better. In the glow of the lamplight I had asked my Mother, "Why can't I sleep in your room?" It was a good question in its own right, showing that I trusted her to protect me. But in the dark, that babyish trust turned restless and then urgent. *"Why?"* became simply *"You!"* No other hope existed in the world: only the light under my parents' door.

During the last few days, both of my children have been scared to fall asleep alone. My older daughter has read Jesus' prophecy in Mark about the end of the world. Tonight, when I've finally found a quiet minute to talk with my husband, she yells for me, "Mama!" I get up from the couch (complaining) and go to her room to comfort her. In a bumbling way, I try to explain all the things I want to write about here. I tell her how important it is for us to call out to God for help; I tell her that he takes care of us and that nothing can ever separate us from his love. I quote a long Bible passage to that effect—

"Okay!" She interrupts me. "I got it, I got it." She folds her arms over her quilt, then scans the room with a wide, nervous stare. She looks at the closet door and sighs. I wonder what nightmarish thing she imagines behind it.

"Could you please stay for a minute?" she asks, showing faith much stronger than mine. She knows unconsciously what I'm working so hard to remember.

"For a few minutes," I say, and stretch out beside her till I know she's asleep.

2
god
from the other side

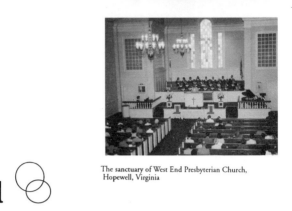

The sanctuary of West End Presbyterian Church, Hopewell, Virginia

It was to be trampled on by men that I was born into this world.
It was to share men's pain that I carried my cross.
—Shusaku Endo, *Silence*

My father, in spite of being a Reformed Presbyterian, gave lots of altar calls. When I was little, we had about as many altar calls as the Southern Baptists. Every other week or so Daddy invited people in the congregation to accept Jesus into their hearts. Sometimes he used the words, "Come to the cross," which meant, in a physical sense, to come up front and pray with him to be saved or else to repent of sin. It seems to me now that I got up and went forward each time the call came. Sometimes I went all by myself, other times with the girl who had a hole in her heart and wore the same white crocheted shawl every week. We marched past the pastel stained-glass windows and pews, all the way to the Remembrance table with the cross sitting on it, toward the man in the seersucker suit, who happened to be my father. I wonder now how he felt about seeing me come every week.

I don't guess I was very good advertising for his evangelism methods.

We heard a lot about the cross at church: "Let us then trust in Jesus' shed blood on the cross," "Take up your cross and follow Christ," "Leave your burden at the cross." We sang about it in many of our hymns:

> *On a hill far away, stood an old rugged cross,*
> *The emblem of suff'ring and shame . . .* *

> *At the cross, at the cross where I first saw the light,*
> *And the burden of my heart rolled away . . .* **

We thought of that cross, first of all, as the literal place of Jesus' death. We'd heard again and again about the agony of crucifixion. Sometimes we felt as if we'd actually been at Golgotha to see Jesus die. Where would we have stood in the crowd? With Jesus' disciples or with his persecutors? It didn't matter, because the cross had become not our condemnation but our salvation: it was the place where we laid down the weight of our sins and took up Jesus' righteousness. This laying down was right at the heart of our evangelical Christianity. When we casually spoke about the "gospel," we referred to the fact that Christ had accepted the heavy blame for sin and paid the penalty for it, so that we no longer had to drag our guilt around like a steamer trunk, only to be pulled down by it into the bowels of hell. *My chains fell off,* went one of our greatest songs, *my heart was free, I rose, went forth, and followed Thee. . . .* We sang those mighty words Sunday after Sunday, so many voices joined in beautiful thunder. *No condemnation now I dread: Jesus, and all in him, is mine! Alive in him, my living Head, And clothed in righteousness divine.****

This freedom really was extraordinary news for many people, especially those who heard it for the first time as adults. They wandered into church (or maybe back to church) after a life of shame and guilt. At the cross, they found their burdens lifted. Hallelujah! But there was a problem: Could the whole thing still apply if you were raised in a devout family—especially a Presbyterian family? If you were baptized while still a baby, if you were taught to believe in Jesus and then made a "profession of faith" at the age of three or four (or even nine or ten), when and by what means exactly did you become aware of your guilt? Christ had supposedly taken that burden off your shoulders before you were old enough to understand how heavy it could get. And if you never felt the weight of sin, could you really feel grateful to Jesus for relieving you of it? How could you understand the gospel—that great cycle of sin/repentance/forgiveness that lies at the heart of Christian life?

There was, of course, the matter of ongoing sin—sin that needed to be confessed and repented of, every day. All baptized, saved children had plenty of it. But even if you believed that you were a sinner, and wanted to repent, your experience of repentance never quite meshed with what you heard preached at church. For example, I learned at church that my sin grieved God and that I should be sorry and ask forgiveness. But I learned at home that, while my mother told me I should be sorry for grieving God by refusing to eat my peanut butter sandwich, I could make her stop talking and give me a jelly donut simply by *seeming* repentant. I wondered why my sin didn't move me to real grief; I decided not to worry about it. The temptation to manipulate my mother was strong, and anyway, at least I hadn't stolen anything, or taken the Lord's name in vain. Those were the bad sins, which I (a devout child of the Covenant, a small Pharisee) would probably never commit. I was inoculated against them the way other children were inoculated against smallpox and rubella.

As often as I heard the gospel preached as a child, I didn't quite get it. From the beginning I saw God not so much in the role of Redeemer as *Rescuer.* God was my hero, my protector from all things terrifying in the middle of the night, whether visible or invisible. When I prayed to Jesus for safety, I saw him not as a suffering Savior, but as a mighty defender—more or less a divine extension of my mother. Naturally, then, my mother also became my image of divinity during the day. As portrayed by Mama, God was a selfless servant of small children, old people, and rowdy teenagers. He was a busy and efficient world manager who held everything together with tireless attention.

For how many unremembered and half-remembered days did Mama and my grandmother and I stay at home together while the rest of the family disappeared to work and school? A blanket of quiet fell over us as the door slammed behind the last pair of feet. Grandma sighed and went to her rocking chair by the front window, staring with sad, teary eyes at the passing traffic. She'd come from upstate New York to live with us (following a bad stroke) and never adjusted to the change; she seemed restless and unhappy. Mama, on the other hand, was busy and cheerful. Mornings sent her into high gear. The day was young! With the cool air blowing up the light yellow curtains, she baked and washed and sewed our clothes, telephoned the needy and the depressed, paid the bills, prepared Sunday school and women's prayer circle lessons, kept up with twenty different correspondents, and above all cleaned the house: top to bottom, mold spores to mildew, dust to dry rot, world without end. Her energy was godlike, Herculean. I followed her around, a small worshiper, doing everything she did in miniature. I had my own Dr Pepper bottle with a sprinkler stuck in the top for wetting the clothes before ironing them on my plastic board. I had my own clothesline and mop and broom. I had my own small hutch and set of yellow plastic dishes. I had my own little Bible. I even had my own small person, an imaginary friend named Pangie, who followed me around doing all the same things on an even smaller scale.

When Mama stopped work, she sat down to the piano to play hymns by ear, then dropped into bed for a nap. I lay down with her but didn't sleep too much. I stared at her large, lumpy stocking feet. I pulled her toes and poked her bunions. She snored patiently. Then once she woke up, we started the whole process all over again, only stopping to pick up my brothers and sister from school. I couldn't imagine life without Mama. She was so strong, efficient, and attentive to our needs. She was our Rescuer. I never imagined then that she could be sad, or needy, or bored.

I, on the other hand, was *often* bored. There was never enough to do during the day, as far as I was concerned. Our house faced a busy street in Hopewell. We lived near the city's only high school, with cars flying up and down past our front walk. Grandma stayed all morning in the bay window, watching quietly, counting off the slow seconds. In the afternoons she sat in front of the television in her bedroom watching her "stories," bent forward with her nose almost touching the screen.

Sometimes I spent the afternoon with her, sitting on a wooden chair with my legs crossed. We watched *All My Children, General Hospital, As the World Turns,* and *Days of*

Our Lives. Like sands lodged in an hourglass, so were these long, empty hours together. Now Grandma was crying at a TV wedding, leaving our world behind in search of a better one. I looked at her soft, old face and wished I had the power to make her happy in this world. I climbed onto her lap and put my arms around her cool neck. She hugged me and then I kissed her on the cheek and went outside to play. What would it be like to grow old? Did it have to be dull? Lonely? Was life a long line with points of boredom at the beginning and end and furious hard work in the middle?

I couldn't imagine myself sitting around bored when I was grown up. I dreamed of busy days and adventures ahead—having a life somewhat like the life of Mama, except without the housework. A life of drama and hard work, with plenty of romance thrown in. American Indians were my great passion of the moment. I wanted to ride a horse one day with a feather stuck in the back of my braided hair; I wanted to wear moccasins and fringe and maybe have a coonskin cap like Daniel Boone (my TV hero). I sure as anything didn't want to end up hopeless and teary-eyed all the time like my Grandma, constantly thinking about some place in the past I couldn't get back to.

Out on the porch steps or on my tricycle, I sat day-dreaming about Daniel Boone and Indians. I dreamed of blood and death and sacrifice, wars between tribes, the last minute rescues of Cherokee maidens. We had a plum tree in the front yard with blood red plums that were good for drawing pictures on the driveway. I drew Indian braves in profile, with braided hair and war paint. I climbed the plum tree, and sometimes the lantern post right next to the road: from there I'd look over at Mrs. Slovac's tiny house across the street. She was an immigrant from Eastern Europe, older than my grandmother, living all alone. Mama often took me to visit her.

One afternoon I'd sat with my legs dangling from a chair, eating fishy-tasting crackers while Mrs. Slovac cried and cried and said things in her native language and my mother comforted her. What was Mrs. Slovac crying about? Impossible for a small child to tell. She was Catholic, and on the table in front of us sat a metal crucifix hovering over a little dish of holy water. I'd never seen anything quite like it. I ran my fingers over the dying figure of Jesus and thought it was beautiful but strange, too. I'd seen lots of pictures of Christ on the cross, but never a statue. I thought that there was something terrible about being able to turn the cross around and see Christ from behind: amazing, and yet sad, too. When the dish of water was empty, I could hold Jesus' anguished face up to my curious eyes and stare straight into, or at, his open eyes, observing every streak of tarnish on his silver shoulders. Christ wracked by pain, looking sadly out into the world.

My understanding of Jesus was still very limited, but my passion was great. I knew that he had been a child once, and then grown up into a man. I believed that he was the Son of God and that he'd died on the cross and had come back to life. The face of Christ on my child's picture Bible had been scratched off somehow, so one day I took a pencil and tried to draw in the best profile of him that I could, which meant that Jesus came out with a pointy head and a beak, like a blue jay. Inside the book, I found no detailed painting of the crucifixion, only a silhouette of three crosses on a hill. That didn't satisfy me: I wanted to see the crucifixion up close. I really wanted a statue like Mrs. Slovac's, but my mother said that Protestants couldn't have such things, so I made do with a picture from *The Encyclopedia of World Religions* on the bookshelf in our living room. It showed a yellow, emaciated Jesus hung up like the carcass of an animal with blackish streams of blood dripping down his bony arms. It was a hideous picture: I would no more show it to my own children than have them watch *The Texas Chainsaw Massacre* just before bed. But that picture drew me again and again. I felt fiercely sad and yet warmed down to my bones, looking at Christ's awful suffering. Such cruelty and love: could the world contain it all and not come apart? I touched the page and felt the glossy paper under my fingertips. I got out my markers and paper and sat down with my legs stretched under the marble-topped coffee table, looking at the book, wanting to draw the picture as I saw it. I liked to draw, but I was still clumsy with a pencil and Jesus' feet came out looking like a pair of cow udders. I went to my mother and asked her: "Could you please draw this for me?"

Mama sat at the round-topped table in the basement, using a yardstick to get the lines of the cross perfectly straight on a piece of posterboard. The human figure was beyond her. After a few erasures, I went to my brother Matt. He drew Christ hanging on Mama's cross with his head bent down and his knees pushed to one side, like in the *Encyclopedia of World Religions*.

Still, something was missing. I found a red marker and went to work, lovingly adding rosy sores and lacerations, broad streams of blood from hands and feet.

I took the poster drawing to kindergarten show-and-tell the next day and stood up in front of Mrs. Burnley's class. "Jesus died on the cross to save us from our sins. This is the blood and here are the nails and the hole where they stabbed him with a spear."

Mrs. Burnley was a sparkly-eyed lady who claimed to be a descendant of Thomas Jefferson. "Thank you, Betty," she said. "That's a *very* vivid picture."

At the front of our own church stood a shiny gold cross. Like all Protestant crosses it was empty. My father hovered over the empty cross each week, delivering the sermon—the focal point of the Presbyterian service, the "pinnacle" of worship. I liked to sit on the front pew, especially on Sunday nights, and hang on his words, or at least the words that wove themselves into jokes and stories. When I lost the connecting threads, though, and the words became abstractions, I opened my eyes wide without blinking and stared. I stared straight ahead until the red carpet of the sanctuary went gold, and the white of the walls went purple, and the gold cross turned red and dripped down over the table it sat on, into the carved words, "This Do in Remembrance of Me."

What were we supposed to do? What were we supposed to remember about Jesus? I was barely old enough to read the words. I wasn't quite old enough to take Communion yet, though, and of course knew nothing about the doctrinal arguments over the meaning of the Lord's Table: whether the bread and wine (Wonder Bread and Welch's Grape Juice) were only symbols of Jesus' sacrifice for us, or whether they mysteriously became his body—actual food for the sustenance of his church. Still, I understood from stories and pictures that Jesus loved us and that he'd died to *rescue* us from sin. Rescue meant something to me, since I so often had need of rescue, and my mother so often provided it. I also understood that Jesus listened to our prayers and cared when we were hurting. Of course I would remember Jesus—heroic, rescuing, caring Jesus.

One Sunday after church, we all sat at dinner around the mahogany table in our dining room, eating pot roast and drinking sweet tea with specks of mint leaves floating on the ice at the top. My brothers and sisters shouted over each in silly laughter. When I'd finished, I asked to be excused and then wandered out into the sunshine to play. I picked up my jump rope from the carport steps and skipped a few times under the plum tree. Then I stared up at the lamppost, with its short bars across the top like the arms of a stick figure or a cross.

Inspiration fell upon me suddenly; who knows where it came from. There was no logic to it. I simply decided to hang myself on the lamppost with the rope. I shimmied up the pole and spent a few moments trying to tie my arms to the crossbars. It wouldn't work. I couldn't quite do all this right side up, so instead I held on and flipped over, upside down, so that I hung on by my knees. After a little bit of a struggle, I managed to tie myself to the pole by my ankles and dangle there, smiling. I stayed that way for about a minute, my skinny white arms loose like bare vines, my fingertips in the grass. My glasses fell down my forehead and got caught in my hair. My shirt slunk down my belly so that my ribs stuck out and my breastbone showed.

I remember feeling joyful. For several more happy seconds I simply pleasured in swinging free, the grass tickling my knuckles, the sky drifting over my toes. It was a lazy, warm day. I swung back and forth a little and then decided it was time to raise myself up again. I tried but couldn't do it. I tried a second time and a third time. I looked up at my bare feet straining out against the sky, but I couldn't reach them. The rope had started to burn my ankles.

Still, I didn't panic. I leaned back against the cool black pole, ready to try again, and then I heard a swishing noise. I twisted my head around to look at the street. A long, large car pulled up beside me; a plump female face pressed itself to the window—upside-down, of course. I could make out that the face was frowning. I smiled and waved: "I'm OK!" I heard a car door slam. Then I heard voices behind me and twisted my head around to see my sister and brothers in motion. They hung by their feet on a green sky. They were agile and quick as acrobats: they climbed over to me from the carport door, not even falling into the clouds below.

"What are you doing? Are you crazy? She's crazy!"

Forever I'll see those faces, the woman in the car and my family, my brothers and sister and parents, their arms out, coming toward me across the grass. They untied me and pulled me from the pole. They asked me what I was doing. I didn't know what to tell them. I fixed my glasses back down on my nose and pulled down my shirt. I told them I'd been pretending to be Daniel Boone.

And it may have been true. I think, though, that I was also playing at the cross, remembering Jesus, trying to *show the Lord's death till he comes.* Although I loved the story of Christ's death, I could only see it through the eyes of a well-loved child. I hardly knew what suffering was. Blood took its color from plums in the front yard; a cross was a place you climbed up to by yourself. Here my family came now to rescue me from my own little cross—dust me off, set me up straight, spank me soundly, and send me off to play.

Six years ago, on a November night, my children were playing with my husband at home. It was dark and cold. I got into my car after an argument with a friend, feeling miserable and utterly lonely. I wanted so much to die. I crossed a small bridge over the Little Cahaba River and looked up at a telephone pole standing erect on the other side. There it stood, straight ahead, glowing red in my headlights. Then, as never before or since, I felt tempted by death. I wanted to race my car into that pole and hurt myself—lacerate myself, bruise myself, crush bones, tear flesh. If I was lucky enough, I'd die quickly and that would be the end of everything.

I'd found my real cross at last, and it was no adventure. Jesus' cross is a place we comprehend best in our hopelessness, when we suffer alone. It's my grandmother's seat in the window—a place of homesickness and wasted days. It's Mrs. Slovac's kitchen across the street, where she dreamed of a lost family and a lost country. The cross is shame and abandonment, exile and humiliation.

And Jesus felt this. He carved out the way of suffering before us. Though he was our rescuer, our redeemer, he was also the man who shared our sorrows. Before he went to the cross, he knelt in darkness and said these words:

My soul is exceedingly sorrowful unto death. . . .****

And later:

My God, my God, why hast thou forsaken me?*****

"My God," he said, "why?" Why should all the unexplainable, excruciating miseries of the world be shoveled into one man's heart like corpses into an oven?

Why, my God, my God?

I remember rolling Mrs. Slovac's crucifix around in my hands, curious and embarrassed. How could I have understood? I didn't know that when we suffer—whether we endure the concentrated suffering of real persecution or the agony of sickness or want—we're given the chance to die with Jesus, to see the world as he saw it from the cross, alone and dying. We look out over his shoulder and see the tragedy of evil. We walk around the back of God and grieve with him from the other side.

3

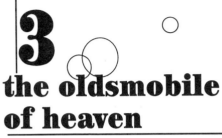

the oldsmobile
of heaven

Remember Lot's wife. Whosoever shall seek to save his life shall lose it; and whosoever shall lose his life shall preserve it.

—Luke 17:32–33

How does the child who thinks of God as all-seeing, all-knowing, all-powerful, grow into the woman who identifies with—even takes comfort in—Jesus' helplessness on the cross? Actually, how does anybody learn to do this?

Children don't come into the world dreaming of surrender and self-sacrifice. They're born with an instinct to survive and control. Some say it's the result of millennia of human evolution, others say that it came with the fall of mankind. Either way, few of us, by nature, identify with the helpless and suffering. Though we may stoop to help people in need, we don't want to suffer, ourselves.

But the cross forces us to suffer. To understand it, we have to feel the pain of it: we have to step away from the world and stand in the darkness with Jesus. This is a place I would never have come to willingly, or without having made wide circles around it first. Long before I came, I sensed the darkness ahead, and I feared it, wishing I could find another way.

As a little girl, I romanticized heroic suffering, the kind I could act out in daydreams and games. Actual pain, though, terrified me. Like so many children who grow up safe and happy, I had a disproportionate sense of impending doom. Lightning would certainly hit *our* house; an escaped convict would make his way to our door; an eye infection would leave me blind. Maybe I spent too much time with my Grandma Van Voorhis, who was a fountain of tragedy: "Don't ever ride your bicycle on the wrong side of the road, Betty. I knew a boy who got hung up on the bumper of a delivery truck and it carried him four miles down the highway before anybody saw him waving his hands. Oh, that was a terrible thing. . . ."

Grandma Van Voorhis had lost her second son, Arnold, when he was still a teenager. She and my mother missed him terribly. They talked about his gentle nature and sense of humor; they recited his accomplishments in dramatics and basketball. I grew up thinking of Uncle Arnold as our family saint: a combination of Shakespeare, Abraham Lincoln, and Larry Bird.

In Mama's high school graduation picture, she looked out from under her cap and tassel with sorrowful eyes. "I had that photograph taken right after Arnold died," she told me, her voice trembling slightly. "My brother and I were best friends. We were only a year apart." Arnold had been dead for nearly thirty years now, but because of all I'd heard about him, he felt more real to me than some of my living relatives whom I'd hardly seen.

Daddy's family, in contrast to Mama's, were practical and unsentimental. My Grandmother Smartt lived on Lookout Mountain in Tennessee, where we'd visited her a couple of times since I'd been born. We called her "Mom" rather than "Grandmother," but she seemed ancient to me. She had a gravelly chuckle and chin hair that scratched when I kissed her. She was like Lookout Mountain itself, hovering above us with layers of wrinkled strata around her bright eyes and down the backs of her hands. I couldn't imagine that she'd ever been young, but Daddy brought out an old, sepia-toned portrait of a little girl and said, "There she is! Who does she look like?"

"Like Betty!" everyone said.

"That's because Betty's the spitting image of her," he said, looking happily between me and the bright-eyed child in the picture. Daddy loved his mother. He told us stories of her adventures in turn-of-the-century Chattanooga: how she tasted the first Coca-Cola served in the city, how she grew up in her father's hotel, the Read House (now a Chattanooga landmark), chauffeured him around town, and parked the car in the lobby on rainy nights. He also told us the legend of himself—how he, Kennedy Smartt, came to be a preacher on account of a family tragedy that God turned to good.

In 1924, he said, a few months before he was born, his parents lost their third child in a terrible accident. The little girl had wandered away to play one day and somehow come to a bluff on the East Brow of Lookout Mountain. There was no guardrail: she fell one hundred feet and died before anyone could reach her. My grandparents didn't speak much of the accident. They didn't weep in public. Something changed in them, though, because for the first time they began going regularly to church. My grandmother quietly dedicated her unborn child to God to be a pastor. She never told Daddy that she'd chosen him for this fate until he was grown and in the ministry.

Because I'd been named for the dead girl, my Aunt Betty, I took great interest in her story. Though she'd died forty-one years before my birth, in our old family pictures she was forever a plump, light-haired little girl, never growing or changing. It was her family that had done all the changing and growing following her death. Changes had tumbled down like loose rock after Aunt Betty died, until, at least in my father's Presbyterian rendering of the story, it became clear that the fall itself was part of God's greater will for all of us. Her death was the catalyst that sent my grandparents to church, that sent him (my father) into the ministry, and that determined we'd become a family of devout believers.

I saw two kinds of death reflected in my aunt's fall. One death came as the fruit of an adventure. It was the tragic but heroic end I'd looked for on the lamppost: the adventurer risked a fall for the joy of the adventure, the ascent. She climbed a bluff, she played fearlessly on the cliff edge, trusting to slender trees and the open sky. When she lost her foothold and slipped, she fell straight into the will, the very purposes, of God: "He that loseth his life for my sake," said Jesus, "shall find it."*

The other kind of death, though, was pointless. It came by accident rather than choice. I dreamed one night that my father and I were in a dark cellar underneath the church, climbing a ladder hundreds of stories high. Suddenly I fell away from him. I tried to grab his hand. I wanted to hold on, but I couldn't. "Help me!" I shouted. But I was gone, straight down into the dark. The idea of separation and darkness, of losing all connection to the world I knew, sent me into a panic. I lay awake nights worrying about it. How would I die? Would I drown? Would I fall off a cliff? Would our house catch on fire? Would I get sick? Would somebody sneak in my window at night and stab me?

These were the days of the Cold War. People thought and talked a lot about the Soviet Union, Red China, the war in Vietnam, the moral disintegration of America, and the eventual end of everything. On television, I saw a show about the atomic bomb, and the mushroom cloud over Japan looked to me like the gray smoke that poured out of the stacks in our factory town. My friends said that the fish were dying in the James River. The foam from the chemicals and the bones of dead creatures were washing up all around Pocahontas's birthplace; the poison in the air was eating away her statue over in the brand new state park not too far from Hopewell. Some people said our air was poisonous. When the wind blew the wrong way, our whole city smelled like rotten eggs. How could things go on like this? Would we die from a hydrogen bomb blast, or from air pollution? I asked my parents, but they didn't seem worried about that stuff.

"Don't think so much about the future," they said, shaking their heads. "Jesus will come back soon."

One evening when the sun was falling behind Mrs. Slovac's roof, I saw a pair of white lines across the orange sky. "Daddy!" I yelled. "Daddy!" I ran and found him mowing grass in the front yard. He cut off the mower. He smelled like sweat and damp grass.

"Look up there!" I said. "Is that Jesus?"

He peered up, squinting in earnest, with his lower lip stuck out. The jet trails inched along the violet sky, into the orange sunset.

"Is that him?"

"No," he said, "that's not him yet. That's a couple of jets."

"Well, could it have been him?"

"Yes, it could have been him. Any day now, he'll be coming back." Daddy cut the mower on again.

I went inside and sat down, satisfied, until I thought, *What if those streaks are coming from Russian jets? What if the Russians are going to bomb us, bomb Richmond?* If not today, then maybe tomorrow. The world was going to end in one of two ways: either with a trumpet blast or with a mushroom cloud. Here again were the two deaths: one a joyous climb and a tumble into God's arms, with angels singing and crowds cheering—not death at all, but a step into new life; the other death a fall that ended in oblivion: separation, pointlessness, and finality.

It wasn't too long after this that I had a new revelation: that heroism and pointlessness might intersect in some other, more difficult place. My best friend now was Gail Sims. She lived a couple of streets away, in a little house with a chain link fence and a big magnolia tree in the back. Gail said her family mostly went to the Church of Christ.

"I go to the Church of Christ, too," I said, standing by her gate, tracing the cracks in the pavement with my bare toe.

"Well, I've never seen you there."

"I go there every Sunday."

"To the Church of Christ?"

"Of course it's the Church of Christ. What else kind of church would it be?"

"You don't go there, because I've never seen you, and my mother plays the piano there."

I didn't know what she was talking about. I knew our church was the Church of Christ. The Presbyterian Church of Christ. And I knew her mother didn't play piano there, because Mrs. Betty Harrison played the piano. So I kept arguing. "She does not."

We went inside and asked her mother who was right. Gail's mother sat slumped over in a chair by the back window, having her afternoon cocktail and cigarette. Her legs were bare white under her skirt. There were dark circles under her eyes. She smiled and looked at us sleepily. "Why don't you come with us to church tonight?" she said to me in a tired, thick voice. "You haven't been to our church before. You can see for yourself."

I'd never been to any church other than mine until that evening. I might have been visiting a foreign country. The little sanctuary fascinated me: the baptismal behind heavy, plush red curtains, the tinny voices of the old ladies behind us, the sight of Gail's mother hunched over at the piano. Her face was sad. After the singing time, a man announced a special class to be held for children while the adults prayed and preached. It was a summer night and still bright outside. A woman took us out a back door to the church lawn, sat us on the grass, and taught us a song about the end of the world, when the Christians would be caught up to heaven with Jesus and the not-Christians left on earth:

> *Life was filled with guns and war*
> *and all of us got trampled on the floor*
> *I wish we'd all been ready*

> *Children died the days grew cold*
> *a piece of bread could buy a bag of gold*
> *I wish we'd all been ready*

> *There's no time to change your mind*
> *the Son has come and you've been left behind*

> *A man and wife asleep in bed*
> *she hears a noise and turns her head he's gone*
> *I wish we'd all been ready*

> *Two men walking up a hill*
> *one disappears and one's left standing still*
> *I wish we'd all been ready*

> *There's no time to change your mind*
> *the Son has come and you've been left behind. . . .* **

I pictured Gail's mother lying in bed, in the dark. She heard a rushing, windy sound beside her and turned to see only a dent left on the pillow where her husband's head had been. What if that were me left all alone? What if I turned to talk to my mother and found that she'd disappeared? What if my whole family had disappeared? Daddy, Grandma, Matt, Danny, Ellen, Mama, everybody? Only me left in the house.

At my own church, I felt safe and comfortable. On Sunday evenings, we all sat on one side of the sanctuary. We were a small, close-knit congregation then, with my father standing up in front of us at a podium, teaching. I was at home here: I imagined heaven being like this, with your friends gathered close around. Yet more and more often now, I sensed that danger could encroach upon us even in the safety of church. I found some cartoon tracts on a stand in the vestibule that offered scary vignettes about the evils of the world and what might happen to people who didn't accept Jesus before he came back to earth. I read them under my desk during Sunday school. Their picture of the end was grim. For those not caught up to heaven in the Rapture, there'd be persecution, famine, disease, widespread demon possession—everything I could imagine and some things beyond my imagination.

My father preached a series of Sunday night sermons on the end of the world that was so terrifying, I had to get up one evening and leave the sanctuary. I went out into the vestibule, sat up on a red-cushioned chair, and watched him from behind the glass windows. I could hear him over the public address system. He said that one day, even before the Rapture, the Soviets might storm the city of Hopewell, Virginia, and take possession of West End Presbyterian. I pictured soldiers marching down the center aisle in olive green clothes and enormous, flat caps, lining up across the front with rifles against their chests. "Do you want to live?" they asked each of us in turn.

"Yes."

"Then spit on Jesus. Curse him. Say there's no God."

"I cannot do that."

"Then you will die."

In terror, I asked Jesus into my heart again and again, hoping I wouldn't deny Jesus before the Soviets, trying to have faith. Hope was that impossible place where adventure and pointlessness (the two deaths) met: I had to be willing to step into death and hope that a new life waited—*hope* I landed in heaven. But not having seen heaven, how could I really hope for it? Or even believe in it? I was expected to throw away this life for the sake of Jesus, who promised a mysterious new life—and what a gamble!

My hope—my faith—was weak. On the one hand, I did want to stand up for Jesus. It made me swell with pride to think about refusing to dishonor him. Oh yes, yes, yes, I wanted to show the world how good he was, and how much

I loved him. I wanted to be the girl who tossed away my life for God. But on the other hand, oh no, no, no, I didn't really want death or even heaven or even Jesus, if it came right down to it: not if having Jesus meant saying good-bye to the world and embracing the unknown. The more I thought about it, the more I feared slipping away from everything close and familiar. Death scared me, even when I pictured it as a door to heaven. Given the choice between martyrdom and rescue, I'd take rescue: people stopping their cars on the street to help; my brothers and sister running from the house to pull me down from the cross; or, in the case of a Soviet invasion, Marines storming the church and battling back the enemy.

One day after school, I disobeyed my mother. Gail had come home with us and it was now time for her to leave. I begged to walk her home.

"Walk her to her house," Mama said, "and then come straight back."

"But why can't I play?"

"Come straight back."

I went down the long porch steps and across the backyard, feeling very disappointed. Gail went with me. We cut between the brick shed and the honeysuckle bushes in the corner of the yard, threaded Mr. Harshbarger's rose bushes and vegetable plots, and skipped around his big yellow house, finally arriving at Gail's street.

Suddenly we felt sunny again. She lived a block down on the corner of City Point Road. We walked that way, stopping every few steps to climb the crape myrtles, their branches smooth like long, graceful arms. We reached her house and hung on the fence for a while, talking.

"Want to have cocktails?" Gail said.

"*Cocktails?* What's that?"

"It's drinks you have at three o'clock."

"OK, sure."

We went inside, into the bright kitchen. Her mother wasn't home today. Gail brought a bottle of ginger ale out of the refrigerator. She poured it into martini glasses for us and put cherries in it. Then we went outside and sat in the shade of the big magnolia tree, shaking ants out of the sweet, white blossoms. I'd forgotten all about being long overdue at home. When I was thinking of getting on my way, Gail's older sister Tammy appeared.

"What are you two doing?" she said in a sly voice.

Tammy was my sister Ellen's best friend. She was thirteen or fourteen. She had long legs and long brown hair that sprouted from the sides of her forehead in heavy pigtails and draped down the front of her blouse, over her new breasts.

"We're playing," we said.

"Do you want to see a secret place?"

"Yes," we said, which was a dangerous answer to a dangerous question.

"You've got to come on a walk with me."

Gail and I followed Tammy out the door and down one street, then another, deeper and deeper into the neighborhood. We followed her to a tall hedge, then through an arbor to a dirt yard where a new house was being framed in. The construction crew had left for the time being. Loose sandpaper and brown mortar sacks blew all around the yard and piled against one wall of the house, the detritus of construction.

"Where's the surprise, Tammy?" asked Gail.

"This is it."

"A house?"

"Not just a house, a half-built house."

"But are we *allowed* to play here?"

Tammy looked disgusted. "If you're afraid, you can go home, little girls."

We looked at each other: we were afraid, but of course we weren't going home. We began to pick through the junk, searching for something to make the trip worth it— maybe an earring or a playing card. All we found were cigarette butts and soda can tabs. But there was something nice about being back here, surrounded by the rich green hedge. A big oak tree stretched its arms over us, creating such deep shade that I didn't notice how the sky was growing darker. I played tag with Gail, jumping over piles of plywood. Meanwhile Tammy stood at the arbor entrance, listening to something.

"My gosh," I said, suddenly realizing what I should have known all along, "I have to go home! I was supposed to go home right away!" I started for the arbor.

Tammy stepped in front of me. She had an odd look in her eye. "You can't go," she said.

"Why not?"

"Listen," she said, and gestured up, over the hedge. I lifted my chin. From somewhere down the street came a crashing sound. *Crash, crash, boom. Crash, crash, boom. Crash, crash, boom.*

"What's that?" I said.

"That," she piped back in a shrill voice, "is the *Russians* coming for you."

"No it's not."

"Yes it is. I didn't want to tell you till we got here, but I brought you here to protect you."

"I want to go home!" Gail said.

"You can't."

Gail screamed. I tried to push past Tammy, but she yelled and pulled me back onto a mound of tracked-up dirt. She gripped me tight around the wrists with her wiry hands. Her head bent forward, her brown hair fell across my shoulder.

"I've got to protect you," she hissed. "They're marching in right now. That's their drums."

"I have to go home."

"You don't have a home anymore, stupid! They've already killed our parents. They've shot them in the head. They're coming for us now."

Gail and I both began to cry. "What will they do to us?"

"You don't even want to know," said Tammy. "But don't worry. I won't let them get you."

I felt my knees going loose. Tammy hugged our faces against her neck. Her hazel eyes swept over us. "Listen!" she said. "They're getting closer!"

We listened. *Crash, crash, boom. Crash, crash, BOOM.* Yes, they were coming near! My heart started to pound. We were going to die! Nobody would rescue us. I stopped struggling and hung against Tammy, breathing. For a while we stood there, locked together, and then finally for some unknown reason, the drumbeat, or whatever it was, stopped.

"They're gone," wailed Gail. "Is it safe now? Can we go?"

Tammy laughed and shoved us away. "Little brats! You'd believe anything I told you."

I stared at her, not comprehending.

"Go on home," she said, snickering. She let us loose and then lolled off, toward the hedge, staring at her fingernails. It began to dawn on me that the whole thing had been a lie, a horrible, hellish lie.

"You're mean!" said Gail.

"And you're a dodo," said Tammy over her shoulder. "Go home now. Make like a banana and split."

I could hardly believe I was free. I felt I'd gained the world again. I ran away as fast as I could, down toward Mesa Drive. The sun was setting ahead of me. I saw the traffic racing back and forth at the intersection. Then a familiar white Oldsmobile turned and came slowly, slowly down the road in my direction. It crept like an advancing tank. As the car came closer, I saw my father's face through the windshield.

If I'd been twenty years older, I'd have run, having learned very well over the years that you don't fly to your own destruction; don't lurch forward like a cow into a tornado. Hide!

But in my child's heart, I was happy to see the car. I felt joyful self-surrender—an urge to leap forward and risk everything, if only because I'd been saved from losing everything. For a few horrible minutes a sadistic girl had made me think that the unimaginable was true: that my family was dead or carted away to the Gulag, that our home was burning and all was lost. She'd forced me to look straight into an oblivion as complete as death. And then, in a second, I'd learned that the world was still intact. I picked up my feet and trotted toward the car. I waved at my own, oncoming doom. My father pulled up beside me and rolled down the window.

"Hi," I said.

"Do you know what time it is?" he asked through square white teeth.

"No sir."

"It's six o'clock. Your mother has dinner on the table. And she's worried sick about you."

I opened my mouth to explain about the Russians and Tammy and Gail and the crashing drum beat, but suddenly the whole afternoon seemed hard to defend. I closed my mouth again.

Back in my own bedroom, stretched across my father's hard thigh, I got the worst spanking of my life so far. With every slap of his huge, flat hand I was a little less glad he wasn't dead after all. He left me in my room, sobbing and trying to suck air back into my lungs. After a while, I went to the kitchen and sat down to a hearty meal.

Yes, my family was here. I was here. The spanking hadn't killed me and the Russians were still in Russia. Nobody had been obliterated in a nuclear explosion. The pollution hadn't yet wiped out the trout in the James River, and maybe another day would pass before the end of the world. I was relieved and glad, and yet bitterness was growing in me with every second.

Because I would rather have had a world where I simply went home and ate supper—without the lecture, without the spanking, without the guilt of having worried my mother and father. Who wouldn't prefer dignity to surrender and humiliation? My pride was already telling me I should have walked rather than run to Daddy's car. Yet I'd run, so happy to see him come for me that I didn't consider how much I risked until I actually met him halfway down the street. Stepping into his car, I stepped over a cliff and tumbled headlong into the will and purposes of my father. Only now do I see Daddy's car as the creeping Oldsmobile of heaven, an image of the cross, the terrible death that rescues us from dying all alone.

4

The Smartts, circa 1972
Left to right: Matthew, Betty, Kennedy, Mary, Ellen, Danny

enter the dragon

In order to have complete confidence in karate you must have confidence in what you are learning from your instructor. What you absorb you must practice until it becomes as natural as walking.... The art of karate is by no means a game and must not be taken as such.

—Jerry C. Piddington

During the years when I learned most about God, I never suspected that I was learning anything. I did what came naturally, following my own inclinations and instincts, at least until somebody stepped in the way. I first tasted the joy of worship, for instance, not by sitting through a lot of church services—those taught me only patience and fortitude—but by worshiping people, surrendering myself to one love after another.

How does anyone acquire that sort of runaway passion for God? It doesn't come naturally. If I'd instinctively loved God the way I loved so many people, I'd have walked on water and raised the dead. But loving people gave me a taste for love itself. I was like a vinca vine that grows along steadily even in the shade: when it finds the sun, it sends out clouds of new green shoots and starlike blossoms. My human loves carried me into the love of God.

From the very beginning, love grew over and under and out of my heart. As a two-year-old I put my arms out to strange men in the grocery store: "Take me to your house! Show me where you live!" When I was six I grabbed a bridegroom around his leg and made him drag me down the church steps to the honeymoon car. Somebody had to disattach my fingers from his tuxedo leg before he and the bride could drive away.

The people I loved so passionately were usually years, even decades, older than I was. Once I begged to give a baby shower for a woman who gave me drawing lessons. She had become my favorite of all: Mama balked at first, but eventually she helped me make a cake and decorate it with a pretty umbrella and ABC blocks. I invited my current best friend, Laura, and her brother Larry. We played party games in my basement and then presented the pregnant woman with baby gifts. Later I got a "thank you" note telling me how special I was to her. In my mind, this meant that the older woman valued me as a friend and equal rather than a child. When her baby girl came along, I saw myself as a kind of second mother to her. I changed her diapers and fed her creamed peas from a dish with expert care. I wanted her to call me

"Aunt Betty," but the family moved away before she learned how to say anything but "cookie."

My own family, the people I loved most and most avidly worshiped, changed a lot during the first ten or eleven years of my life. I measure our changes best in family portraits. A black-and-white photograph from 1967 shows that my brothers are spindly little boys with cropped hair. My sister is small, with an elfish face and a dark bob. I sit on a stool next to her with one leg tucked up under me. My parents dwarf us all, mighty giants, representatives of God, still young and energetic, thoroughly capable. They're ready to handle the moral and spiritual education of sub-thirteen-year-olds. This was the period in which my brother Danny had his mouth washed out with soap for making up a bad word, which sounded something like "blithnop!" or "crit!" Nobody remembers for sure.

In another black-and-white photo, this one from 1972, my brother Matt towers over the rest of us, his thumbs hanging out of the pockets of his button-fly jeans. He leans with his hip out and cocks his head back, his long, smooth hair framing his handsome face. He barely smiles. He's seventeen, and looks like he's pretty sure the whole history of the world is actually the story of him. My brother Danny, fifteen, stands on the other side of the picture, tucked slightly into the background with curly hair, horn-rimmed glasses, and a monogrammed sweater. He looks miserable to be alive. My sister, Ellen, is thirteen. She folds her arms and smiles wisely as if to say, "I'm the only one here who sees through everybody else." As for me, I barely come into the picture at all, my toothless grin showing over the white border at the bottom. Behind us stand my parents: older, smaller, and no longer in charge. God has taken a step down from his throne. Amazing that five years should be enough to humble such a pair of giants, to unmake the wise and valiant and lift up the young and cocky.

Another five years and we are all fuzzy people in a hasty, cropped-together snapshot. The fashions of 1977 do not flatter any of us, but my sister looks downright strange. She appears to be hovering slightly above the couch. The truth is that because my father couldn't find one good picture of all of us, he decided to cut and paste together the imperfect photos that he had. He cut a smiling, seventeen-year-old Ellen out of one photograph and glued her smack-dab over an eyes-closed Ellen in another. Later, when Ellen was home from college, she pulled off the smiling picture and pasted it next to the eyes-closed picture, so that in the snapshot she appeared as twins. But Daddy got hold of it again and reglued Ellen so that as we see her now, she's no longer twins, only sort of weightless and ghostly-looking, like a dead relative hovering over a séance table. Matt appears with a scruffy beard and long hair, home from art school but undoubtedly far away in mind. Danny stares in earnest: he's with us briefly from college in Wheaton, and looks eager to get back. My mother appears worn out with this and that—still probably grieving over my Grandma, who has recently passed away. Daddy wears his plaid Christmas suit and grins from ear to ear in his preacherly way. I sit smiling and keeping my own counsel. What I am thinking here is lost to me now. Maybe I'm in a state of shock.

From the time Matt left for college when I was eight, we grew apart as a family, never to be woven back together again—at least not completely. Like most devout evangelicals, my parents had hoped to create the model Christian home, with model Christian children who grew up reading the Bible, praying, leading other youths to the Lord, and planning to be missionaries or pastors or pastors' wives. But we were ordinary kids, not miniature missionaries. My brother Matt came from East Carolina University one Christmas (maybe the same year we took that bad picture), toting his portfolio with him. I stared with my mother at the artwork spread out for us on the basement Ping-Pong table, wanting to giggle. That was a naked person, wasn't it? A naked woman, drawn from a live model. Mama barely winced, but I knew that under her calm surface was roiling worry. She didn't quite know what to do with my older brothers and sister now that they were no longer children— how to handle the turbulence and outright rebellion of young adults. Her own teenage unhappiness had driven her to Jesus and the life of the Spirit; nothing had prepared her for these children who preferred *Mad Magazine* to *Daily Bread.*

So did the strife at home, the rapid family changes, and the shrinking of my parents push me toward other loves too hard and too soon? I see myself at the bottom of the second family picture, my face looking like a punctuation mark in the story. My older brothers and sister were the real narrative, and I knew it. Sometimes they pulled me into their adventures: Matt took me arrowhead-hunting in Prince George County, Danny taught me to play chess, Ellen woke me up to talk after she slipped into our room late at night. For most of my childhood, though, they lived apart from me. I created my own story, playing by myself and drifting in and out of other families and other lives.

I picture myself again as a ten-year-old giving a baby shower in my basement for a woman I worshiped, adored beyond words. I see the party games on the tile floor, the homemade cards and presents bought with weeks of savings, the mother-to-be with an enormous belly, smiling at the cake I'd baked her, indulging me. I was a natural worshiper—a natural lover—and that would have been fine if I'd naturally loved and worshiped God. Oh, but then who does that? Everybody worships someone other than God. In my case it turned out to be many people.

In the mid-1970s, the martial arts became wildly popular in America. At first we thought it all sounded dangerously un-Christian: we pictured Hare Krishna followers and Mansonites and hippies doing Eastern meditation in communes. But then came the television show *Kung Fu*, and suddenly every kid among us was dreaming of doing flying round kicks in slow motion. My father, always on the lookout for ways to bring more people into the life of the church, agreed to allow a karate class to meet in the gym.

The teacher was a new guy at church, Ralph Atkins, who had an advanced black belt from some famous dojo in California. Seventy-five people showed up on week one. We sat on the bleachers in the stuffy gymnasium, while Sensei Ralph paced before us in his crisp black uniform, teaching us the history and vocabulary of karate. He told us about its Chinese beginnings, its Japanese development, and its American expressions. There was more than one style to all the martial arts, he said. We would learn "soft style" karate, which meant we'd be practicing fluid motions that emphasized grace over strength. Eventually we'd have to practice with boxing gloves—once we got to the stage of sparring and could really hurt each other. Unfortunately, getting that far was going to be hard and probably impossible for most of us. We would be required to do one hundred push-ups and 150 sit-ups every week. We would crouch in the "horse" stance, bowlegged, until we couldn't stand up. We would hold our arms straight out from side to side till we fainted from pain. The easiest part of karate to learn would be the breathing, and even that would be incredibly, impossibly difficult. Through all of this, Ralph would be our lord and master, the monarch of the gym. He would work us to death, without mercy.

"Can I have a couple of assistants to demonstrate something?" he asked.

My hand shot up, but he picked two teenaged boys. They held a board while he kicked it in two. Then he picked a lanky, floppy-armed man out of our ranks and instructed the man to charge him. When the man charged (rather meekly), Ralph put a headlock on him. He said that, if he wanted to, he could kill that man right there, right there in the West End Presbyterian Church gym. I watched, nodding.

At home, I repeated to my mother everything the Sensei had told us. "Our karate motto is 'Check rather than strike, strike rather than maim, maim rather than kill, kill rather than die.'"

"That's fine," said Mama, not listening.

"Sensei Ralph says you can make me my *gi* at home."

"OK." After a second, she looked up. "Make your *what?*"

"Karate clothes."

"I don't know anything about karate clothes! Did you tell him I could make that?"

"He says all you need is a pajama pattern. I have to have it by next week, Mama. I'm going to work my way to black belt."

"Black belt!" She muttered something and shook her head, probably feeling like the cart behind a runaway horse. The next day, though, she dutifully bought the pajama pattern and the white cloth and sewed me a fine-looking *gi*. Since the material was thin, she insisted that I wear a t-shirt under it, though I had nothing yet to hide. Ralph himself gave me an official white belt: I had to loop it around my skinny waist three times to keep the ends from dragging the ground.

It turned out that Ralph's teaching style wasn't a good evangelism method: anybody masochistic enough to attempt a hundred push-ups at a time was probably already a Presbyterian. So, with each passing Tuesday, the class dwindled further and further, till only a handful of us faithful remained. The smaller the class became, though, the more my dedication grew. Karate took over as the driving force of my existence. I worked out every day: I shadowboxed at school, I practiced in the backyard each afternoon in my *gi*, with the light moving over the bright green trees and shining purple through the headband tied around my forehead. The color of my headband meant that I would soon move up to the purple belt, or second rank. I was flexible and had good, high kicks: I could easily do the *katas*—choreographed fight steps. Sensei said I'd be a green belt in no time.

When my brothers came home at Christmas, they were skeptical.

"So what makes karate an art instead of a sport?" said Danny, sarcastically. (He had a high opinion of the arts and a low opinion of sports.)

"Well, it's kind of like ballet," I said. "It has special movements that you have to learn."

"Aren't there special movements in baseball and football?"

"Yeah," I said nervously. "But people are trying to get karate into the Olympics."

"And? That proves it's a sport."

"Yeah, but—you need to talk to Ralph. He'll explain."

"Ralph Atkins is an idiot," said Matt. "Did you hear what he did to Tommy Roberts? He asked Tommy to assist in a demonstration. Then he punched him in the gut without warning him first, and busted an artery. Tommy almost bled to death."

"I guess it would have been for the sake of art," said Danny.

They both rolled their eyes.

I tried to defend the Sensei, but my explanation fell apart, so I pretended to agree with Danny that karate wasn't really an art and with Matt that what had happened to Tommy Roberts was terrible, but secretly I thought that if Ralph said or did something, it had to be right. So what if

Ralph had punched Tommy Roberts? He punched people all the time. You were supposed to be ready for it—either to block it or to take it. Not that he'd ever punched me. As the youngest person left in the class, I was more of a teaching prop than a sparring partner. I'd become his official model for whatever he wanted to demonstrate, whether it was the so-called "killing points" on the human body ("OK, Betty, lift the back of your shirt and let's have a look at those kidneys"), or a way to flip an attacker twice your size over your hip. When it came to flipping attackers, people must have thought I was a child prodigy. Ralph always fell straight to the mat when I flipped him, like a stuffed dummy. Then he got back up and told how he could have killed me if he'd chosen with a blow of one knuckle to my temple.

One day, I met Sensei in the gym before class and watched him demonstrate how to break a pile of five bricks once with a single strike of his hand. This I knew I'd never do, but he told me a trick afterward for breaking one brick at a time. Hold the brick with your left hand and pull it up slightly into your strike. It would work, he said, if I had the courage to hit hard enough. Courage and faith were everything in karate. Breathe deep, let go. I shouldn't worry about breaking my hand. Yeah, I might break it, but it would heal, right? I went home and tried again, again, and again, always afraid to throw myself into it. I examined the tiny bones of my fingers; I flexed the muscles on the sides of my hands to see how hard they were. Could they protect me? Then I hit again, but nothing happened. It seemed impossible.

A few days later, I stared at a brick on the back porch of my house. This would be *the* brick. I knew it would. I was going to give myself to it without holding a single thing back.

I set the brick on the edge of the concrete stoop, lifted my right hand, curled my fingers once in a half-fist, and shouted "*Kiai!*" as I let go with all my strength. Hand, arm, shoulder, chest, thighs: force moved through my body like a spasm.

The world stopped. The brick split in two. Half of it fell and rolled down on the green grass, settling beside my navy blue sneakers.

I jumped up and down. "I did it! I did it! Mama, I did it!" I tore up the back steps, ran through the carport door, and went inside to find my mother. "I did it, Mama, I broke the brick!"

My mother looked at me, amazed. "You're kidding!" She came out to watch me do it all over again: it took me a couple of tries, but finally the second brick split in two like the first. Now I ran to Mr. Harshbarger's yard and called him over from his garden: "You know what I can do, Mr. Harshbarger? I can break a brick in two! Come watch!"

Old Mr. Harshbarger rubbed the stubble on his chin. He'd known me since I was a tiny child. "That's impossible," he said.

My mother came up behind me. "She can really do it," she said proudly. "You should show him, Betty. Show him how you broke that brick."

The three of us walked over the path around Mr. Harshbarger's tool shed and across my yard to the back steps. The old man watched me skeptically, leaning on his rake with one hand, the thumb of his other hand curled in his belt.

"Dear God," I prayed in my head, "let me break this brick." Then I lifted my hand and shouted "*Kiai!*" and felt my hand falling down again right through the baked clay as if it were rotten wood. I broke a third, a fourth, and a fifth brick.

"Well, I never," said Mr. Harshbarger, shaking his head. "I never in a million years. It's a miracle."

"It is a miracle," said my mother.

I wonder now what god I was praying to when I asked to split the brick. I addressed God the Father looking down from heaven, but my real god of the moment was the god of karate, Ralph Atkins. My desire to please Ralph had given me courage and faith—the two qualities he'd said were everything in the small universe of karate—and the fact that my faith bore fruit (I'd broken the brick) only made him more divine in my eyes.

It wasn't that I'd planned to idolize Ralph, or even that I was aware of doing it. But my love for him had all the best qualities of discipleship. I lived by his teaching, I hungered for his approval. I was a congregation of one.

It happened that Ralph himself had very strong opinions on religious matters. He and his wife weren't Presbyterian in background or even inclination: after receiving Jesus at a healing service in California, they'd moved to Virginia and somehow ended up with us. In many ways, they didn't blend well with the rest of the congregation: Ralph's wife wore short, tight skirts and white boots. She was quiet and often looked depressed. As for Ralph, though he seemed to love my father's preaching, it was Jimmy Swaggart he adored above all preachers. "I believe in the gifts of the Spirit," he said, meaning he believed that Christians should be healing the sick and speaking in tongues. He showed me places in the Bible where it implied that speaking in strange tongues was a gift everyone could have for the asking. This was news to me: I was astounded. If Ralph had a gift, then yes, I wanted it too, as I wanted to break bricks and do round kicks. I wanted the Holy Spirit to fill me and bless me and do miracles around me almost as badly as I wanted to learn to spar on a balance beam or twirl nunchaku.

I highlighted every passage in my Bible that related to the gift of tongues and healing. Each morning for some time (a week, maybe two weeks, maybe even three) I woke up and set my alarm clock for twenty minutes. I spent part of that twenty minutes in praise, adoration, confession, petition, and so on, remembering all the things I'd heard in church and from Ralph. I spent the other part either asking for the gift of tongues or sleeping.

"Dear Holy Spirit, I adore you. I adore you so much." I prayed as I'd heard Ralph pray. "I ask that you would really listen to me, and that *if it is your will*, I will speak in the tongues of angels."

While I fervently prayed that prayer, I also held back in fear. I imagined that speaking in tongues would feel strange. An odd sensation would come over me, like hot water spreading over the crown of my head. My eyes would start to flutter. I'd lose control of my body and fall to the ground, helpless. But Ralph promised that tongues wasn't like that at all. Tongues was a wonderful, good thing, he said. It made you smarter rather than stupider, it woke you up instead of putting you to sleep. I believed him, of course, but for me, it still took faith to ask for this gift: not only faith in God, but also faith in Ralph.

Day after day, morning after morning, I prayed fervently for the gift. I kept fearing it, too, and asking God to help me not to fear. But it didn't really matter, because, as hard as I prayed for it, I simply didn't get it. Ralph said the right time would come. The important thing now, he said, was to keep praying, be obedient, and love Jesus. Just look into the face of Jesus and love him. I believed Ralph, but I also wondered whether I loved Jesus enough. And if I did, why didn't he give me what I asked for?

Ralph said that if we really loved God we'd be on fire for the Lord and tell everyone about Jesus. We'd witness up and down the highways and byways of life, spreading the news about salvation to people all over the world. I was anxious to prove my love for Christ and I started thinking I might like to be a missionary. I began to carry chalk around with me and write Bible verses on sidewalks: "Jesus Loves You. Read Your Bible. God is Good. Trust in the Lord with All Thy Heart and Lean Not on Thine Own Understanding." How could a Christian be more on fire than this? How could God not hear my prayers?

During the summer, I heard D. James Kennedy speak at a Bible conference. He challenged us to raise our hands and promise to tell at least one person the good news about Jesus Christ every single day over the next week. So I raised my hand and promised that, yes, for the next seven days I would find someone to accost on the street and preach salvation to. Only, then I forgot I'd promised. Six days later I remembered and realized that I had to find seven people *real quick* and witness to them: it was the only possible way to make up for lost time. So I went from house to house on my bicycle, ringing doorbells, asking people if they'd like a little yellow tract about how to get saved. Sometime around eight-thirty at night, I rode home and parked my bike in the carport. Mama came out on the porch and stood in a square of light from the screen door.

"Where in the world have you been?" she said, her voice shaking. "I've been worried sick."

"I've been handing out tracts and witnessing."

"At this time of night?"

"Yes, at this time of night."

"It's after dark!"

"I promised at the Bible conference. I promised and I didn't want to break my promise." I might as well have said the words of the young Jesus to his parents, when they found him lingering at the temple, conversing with doctors of the law: *How is that ye sought me? wist ye not that I must be about my Father's business?** I felt that spiritual commitments surely trumped earthly ones, and my mission of winning the lost had been more important than the feelings of my family. Ralph would have understood. Mama, however, wasn't impressed. She grounded me from TV for an entire week. I can't remember for sure, but I think I probably took comfort in the words of the Beatitudes:

> *Blessed are ye, when men shall revile you, and persecute you, and shall say all manner of evil against you falsely, for my sake. Rejoice, and be exceeding glad: for great is your reward in heaven: for so persecuted they the prophets which were before you.***

By now, in karate, I was almost a green belt—halfway to black in our particular branch of the martial arts. Ralph gave me a fancy certificate with dragons on it and the new title of "green belt ho." My brothers and sister laughed at this, of course, so I stopped talking about karate around them at all. But when I was away from them, and especially when I was in class, I felt proud. At times, Ralph had me take part of the class off separately and demonstrate basic positions to newcomers.

"Listen," a man said scornfully to me when I'd shown him the correct way to make a fist, "I been punching things all my life and I don't need no little girl to tell me how to do it."

"Yes sir," I said politely, but inwardly I scorned him right back. How could an ordinary mortal pass judgment on me? Only Ralph's opinion counted for anything, and Ralph had affirmed that I was talented and important. I was the disciple and star pupil, the prodigy to the great master.

And then, near the end of the karate year, the unthinkable happened. Ralph hurt his back. Classes were canceled until further notice. For weeks, Ralph was out of work, out of church, and out of karate. I sat at home on Tuesday nights, watching *Happy Days*. What would I do without the Sensei? How would I ever achieve a black belt? How could I be happy when I didn't have him to pursue, to idolize, to adore?

One Saturday, I convinced Mama to let me visit him. She drove me to his apartment after lunch and said she'd pick me up in a few hours. Ralph's wife met me at the door, a fierce look on her face.

"Can I please see the Sensei?" I said.

"Sure you can see him," she said huffily. "You can have him all to yourself. I'm going to work."

I waved Mama on and went in as the car pulled away. I found Ralph lying back in his bedroom on a bare mattress, wearing a black fishnet tank top and a white cloth tied around his forehead. I sat down next to him on the bed, a little embarrassed, but also flattered. His wife came in for a moment and shuffled things around noisily. Then she left again without a word and went out the front door, slamming it behind her.

"She's ticked at me," he said.

"Why?"

"She's tired of me lying on my butt."

"But you hurt your back! You can't even stand up, right?"

He winked at me. "I know that and you know that, but she doesn't believe me."

He began to talk about his wife, how they'd met and married. He told me about the life he'd lived before he got saved. There had been other women, he said. He'd walked down the paths of sin. I imagined him and a beautiful woman talking on his bed, as we were doing then. I looked

at the cords of muscles shining on his raised arms, the brown
blanket balled up at the end of the bed.

"I probably shouldn't be telling you all this," he said.

"Why not?"

"Well you're not really old enough—"

"I understand everything you're saying!"

"No you don't. Not everything."

He was right that he shouldn't have told me those things.
Until now I'd held happily to my child's idea of romantic
love. To love a man was to be like a daughter to him. I'd
pictured Ralph and me kickboxing side by side forever: him
hoisting me up on his shoulders and saying, "She's the best
little green belt I ever trained." Now, alone with my hero, my
god, I sensed dark mysteries ahead that I hadn't thought of
before—grown-up mysteries of sexual jealousy and marital
rage and unfaithfulness.

The afternoon ended. Mama picked me up and asked
me how my visit went.

"Did you have a good time with Mr. and Mrs. Atkins?"
she asked me.

"Yes." I knew better than to tell her Ralph's wife had left
for the rest of the day.

"Are you as interested in karate as you ever were?"

I looked over at her sharply. "Well, why wouldn't I be?
Ralph says I'm going to be a black belt if I keep working at
it. I'm going to try to get a brown belt by next year!"

I meant it. But I never got that brown belt, much less a black. Ralph moved away from Hopewell a few months later to pursue another job. His move brought an end to my karate dreams, my daily devotions, and even my sidewalk chalk ministry. I don't remember ever doing door-to-door evangelism again; I never broke another brick or spoke in tongues. I wrote one letter to Ralph and didn't get an answer.

For a while I missed him, though I never saw him again in such a cloud of glory, so holy and all-knowing. From that day I visited Ralph at home, I felt a vague discomfort. It was as if my eyes had been opened to the possibilities of good and evil: I wished I hadn't loved him so blindly. I thought I'd been silly not to see his shortcomings.

Yet it seems to me now that God wastes no loves, not even foolish and idolatrous affections. While the worship we give to him is often dull mantra, our hearts cry out for someone real to adore—Here! Now! We fall in love, and that love widens the space inside of us. When God does come, our hearts are ready.

I still think of Ralph's favorite hymn. Though at the time I only loved it because he did, it meant much more to me, later:

> *Turn your eyes upon Jesus,*
> *Look full in his wonderful face,*
> *and the things of earth will grow strangely dim*
> *in the light of his glory and grace.* ***

5
face
to face

Betty, 1976

And Jacob was left alone; and there wrestled a man with him until the breaking of the day. And when he saw that he prevailed not against him, he touched the hollow of his thigh; and the hollow of Jacob's thigh was out of joint, as he wrestled with him. And he said, Let me go, for the day breaketh. And he said, I will not let thee go, except thou bless me.

—Genesis 32:24–26

I see now that God was there from the beginning, not only watching and helping but giving me pictures of the path I'd have to walk as an adult. First came lessons in helplessness and self-surrender, then a deluge of desires, so that one day— before I even saw that my longings had changed—I found myself desiring Jesus. But the world is an ambiguous place: if human love gives us an appetite for divine love, it also bruises our hopes, calls forth wants, and then disappoints them again and again. By the time we're ready to love God, our hopes may be worn almost to nothing—a tiny nub, a shiny sliver of longing.

When I was eleven years old, longing was everything. The energy to accomplish anything sprang either from great longing or the strong application of an outside force, such as my mother with a paddling spoon. Since I came from an evangelical family, that same mother often reminded me to do everything "for God's glory," but she might as well have said "Do it for quantum physics," for all the sense that made to me. Self-discipline waited far in the future, along with self-control. I hadn't yet discovered stoicism. Desire was my engine. I thought that, with strong enough desires, I could perform miracles: fly an airplane solo, publish a book, learn Chinese.

What I wanted to do most was run. I used to wake up early some mornings to go jogging with my father. We didn't run every day, or even every week. He traveled too often for a regular routine at home, though I'm sure he found ways to exercise on trips. I imagine him gathering mud on his shoes in Bogota, loping past a shrine near Baghpur. I see him in his orange sweatsuit, a silver-haired man smiling against the pain, waving to people in cars or buses or rickshaws, waving to anyone who passed by.

Because he traveled so much, I never adjusted to the early hours he kept. Some mornings, I'd hear his soft tap on my door and see a thin crack of light from the hallway. He'd already slipped away like a ghost, passing on to the kitchen for a cup of Sanka. I knew he'd go running with me or without me. I could think of a hundred excuses not to get up, the very first being that my bed felt so warm, while outside, at least during fall and winter months, it was so very cold.

On the days I did drag myself from a warm bed into the cold morning, I found my strength in qualities I'd inherited from my father: joy, ego, imagination. I thought of Daddy as a great man, and I wanted to be like him. I knew from books—from biographies of Wilma Rudolph, Jim Ryan, Roger Staubach—that the path to greatness lay through the fields of self-torment. So I got up to torment myself. I put on baby-blue sweats and an extra jacket with a hood. I grabbed a handful of cereal. I already heard the car revving up outside. Daddy would give me just a few more seconds before he left without me.

The particular day I'm remembering must have been in January or February. I went out in the carport and saw the VW at the far end of the driveway, mist spilling over the yellow headlights. The engine rattled in the icy air. I jogged up to the car, waving, and hopped into the passenger's seat. The windshield was frosted up; it glittered like a field of stars. Daddy peered through the circle he had scraped. It was tiny, barely big enough to see through. He liked to take chances with his driving. Sometimes he steered with his knees or glanced at the Bible propped on the wheel.

How crazy to be heading out this early in this kind of weather to do something so painful! There was still time to repent! I thought I could feel a stomachache coming on. I could have used the weak stomach excuse on my father. He wasn't tough on me. He was generous and forgiving, inclined to let people have their way about things as long as it did no harm. I liked how he never pushed me. I liked his calm presence. I liked the way he looked. His lower lip jutted out, slightly, except when he smiled. He walked with a limp, maybe from a shortened leg, or maybe from his war injury. (He'd been shot in Germany when he was nineteen. I'd heard the story in one of his sermons, how a drunk lieutenant sent him on a communications mission straight into an enemy ambush. Daddy stayed in a hospital until the war ended and then went to Austria with the Army of Occupation.)

As far as I was concerned, all fathers walked the way he did, crooked and slightly stooped. His hands were freckled, with a narrow, elegant look, turning out slightly at the wrist when he wrapped his fingers around the black ball of the VW gearshift. Everything about him seemed easy. If I'd told him right then that I couldn't run that morning, he'd have let me sit alone in the cold car, fogging up the windows, and he'd have come back musty and damp after his two miles and taken me home without a critical word. I knew it. What I didn't know was whether he cared one way or the other—whether it mattered to him if I came or not. Why shouldn't he be generous with me, let me have my own way, if he didn't even care?

We parked behind Hopewell High School and walked across a strip of damp brown grass to the track. I felt stiff in the cold. My feet were a pair of sleepers, still numb. We began running while it was dark. Then the sun edged up to the horizon and the world looked like an old photograph, all in gray. Daddy was far away on the opposite curve of the track, jogging along at a steady pace. His orange suit was the first thing to light up in the streak of sun through the trees. I could hear his breathing, but I couldn't catch up to him.

People often say that your ideas about God come from your ideas about your father. The first person who told me this was a professor at Wheaton. I didn't see it then, but I realized later that my picture of God was almost a mirror reflection of Daddy. Both were wise, kind, generous, forgiving, and utterly practical. They were often abroad, and even when home never sat down except on Sunday—and then only after church. They didn't feel pain. They had a particular love for the poor, especially children, and went far out of their way to help people in need. When their anger did boil over, it was something to see; it sent everybody running for shelter.

As a little girl, I worshiped Daddy because he was so strong and so well-respected. People all over town knew him and liked him. The cashier at the drug store would say to me,

"Oh, you're Rev. Smartt's little girl!" and toss a free Hershey bar over the counter. The lady at the bank would load me up with extra suckers. On Sundays, when the nursery workers released me to my family, I ran for Daddy and he took me up in his arms. He carried me draped across his shoulder through the hall, through the crowd of parishioners, to the vestibule. I hated all the talking. Endless, monotonous talking and handshaking, everybody wanting his attention, as if he belonged to them. But the fact that so many people wanted him made it thrilling that he really did belong to me. His voice and his laugh were in my ear. He was mine.

Later I loved him best for his stories: he could tell stories like nobody else. Some of them were melodrama from *Reader's Digest* or *100 Best Illustrations for Sermons*. These included the one about the little girl who was ashamed of the burns on her mother's hands until she learned that her mother got them by climbing into a fiery window to save her as a baby; also the one about the engineer whose little boy got stuck in the gears of a bridge as a passenger train came rolling toward it—like God our Father, this earthly father had to sacrifice his beloved son to save the lives of strangers. Daddy never failed to bring the congregation to tears with the train story, though I figured I'd better stay away from bridge gears.

There on the front pew of the sanctuary, with my bare legs bent over the smooth wood and my feet kicking in shiny shoes, I listened to him tell stories of Daniel and

Nebuchadnezzar, the Medes and the Persians, Alexander the Great. He filled in biblical gaps from his readings in *Ridpath's History of the World*, a behemoth set of Victorian books that had come down to us from my grandparents. Eventually I read those books myself, or tried. I always started at the beginning of the multi-volume set, which meant that I managed to cover the Babylonians and Egyptians several times but never made it to William the Conqueror. Somewhere around college I learned that Ridpath probably hadn't been accurate, anyway, and I felt a giant sense of relief. No need to finish the big books, ever. They were not part of the path to greatness.

Daddy was good with little children. I was closest to him when I was a small child, and it occurs to me that my sister had been the one closest to him not too long before, and my brothers before that, each in his time. I have a photograph of a welcoming reception at our church before I was born. My brother Danny is about five and hangs under Daddy's elbow. Ellen is three and in his arms. Only Matt (who's seven) has moved a little ways off. We all moved away in our own time, we all drifted a little farther out. I guess that's the way it's supposed to be, but when I think about it, it surprises me. What should a child feel, moving away from a father? Should she know that she's separating? Should she grieve over the separation then, or should she recognize it only later, and wonder why she hadn't noticed at the time? And who usually moves first, parent or child?

My father was good in so many ways. He praised me. He laughed at my jokes. In my whole childhood, he gave me barely an unkind word. But he never spent long at home. As our church grew, it occupied more of his attention. He traveled constantly, staying busy with Presbyterian politics, missions, and fundraising. Eventually, he helped give birth to a new denomination of evangelical Presbyterians: The Presbyterian Church in America, Reformed and missions focused. That denomination was his child as much as anything or anybody was his child. Once, when I was twelve, I invented a Presbyterian Church in America Monopoly game. The point of the game was to travel around and around and around and around the board, and then go to the General Assembly once a year, which represented either Jail or Free Parking, according to your point of view.

When I was little, Daddy brought me gifts from his travels: an EtchaSketch, an Indian war bonnet, a tomahawk. I have a postcard that he sent me from Mt. Fuji (what was he doing there, anyway?). One day I stood in our long hallway, on the wood floor, with the ceiling fan roaring above my head, and I looked at the thing he'd brought me home from his most recent trip: a small bag of peanuts. I was about nine years old and I knew the difference between a bag of peanuts and an EtchaSketch. Not long after that came a shampoo sampler from a Holiday Inn in Mississippi, then a bar of soap in a paper wrapper and a plastic bag of tissues. The gifts themselves represented gradual separation. They seemed less and less substantial, like shadowy images broadcast into our house. You could almost hear the fluttery wheels of the projector turning behind my bag of peanuts. You could almost put your hand through the soap.

Daddy himself became the man who was usually gone: the voice on the phone, the occasional disruption in the basement tools. A huge painting of a mountain scene in Georgia sat propped up against the wall in the basement. Could he have painted it? These days I couldn't imagine him staying home long enough to do it. When he did come home, he was like a televised image, a movie starring someone we used to know. I always felt happy to see him, but I'd learned not to expect him to see me. When he did appear and assert his will, I found I resented it. Who was this interfering stranger? The principal of our church school (my father was superintendent) put his arm around me and said, "I'm sorry your daddy has to be gone so much. That must be sad for you." I said cheerfully, "Oh, I don't mind. Then Mama doesn't make me do the dishes."

I understand now my father's love of traveling alone. There's great freedom in being a stranger, a mystery to the world. I can imagine myself happily spending days alone and unknown, walking down a tunnel through an airplane door several times a month, enjoying the bustling anonymity of trains and restaurants and the quiet anonymity of hotel rooms, where you may sleep on a mattress as hard as a rock, but at least you're stripped of social identity and responsibility—Motherhood, Marriage, etc. Some people shed all morality in hotel rooms; other people see God for the first time. I understand both phenomena.

On my refrigerator sit five boxes of cereal with a large window cut out of the back of each. The missing rectangles of cardboard meanwhile lie in a pack under the microwave, wrapped in a rubber band and representing 500 American Airlines Advantage miles (which will be 1000 miles after another five boxes of Cracklin' Oat Bran). My husband and I ate at the Olive Garden one evening and I asked him if he'd mind me going to Italy all by myself sometime. It was like picking at a scab. He doesn't understand why I want to go places alone. Wanting to go to Italy alone; having a happy marriage: the two things appear mutually exclusive.

I explain myself by revisiting my childhood out loud for the twenty-fifth time. How many men have sat across from a wife at a restaurant listening to her analyze herself, thinking, "If I can get her home to bed, it may all be worth it." But even to say that betrays my thinking about men in general. I've conceded to some invisible critic that all men are essentially shallow and incapable of depth. Why expect anything from them? They're dispensable in the emotional economy, like associate vice presidents or senior executive managers.

Yet I see how my daughter reacts to my husband. They play games: basketball, baseball, chess, Monopoly. She comes away crying, her arms wrapped tight around her chest, her red face hidden in her golden hair. What's happened? He's a gentle person by nature: I know he hasn't hurt her intentionally. In fact, watching him react to her is like watching a batter who's accidentally whacked a ball right at the pitcher's head. He stands there amazed, bat still in hand, staring at the figure sprawled out over the mound. How could that have happened? My daughter is crying herself to sleep because Jon beat her at Monopoly. Actually he didn't even beat her: he simply had the nerve to put a hotel on one of his cheap pieces of real estate. But she's crying, and some instinct in me says that her tears don't come from disappointment in the game. She's disappointed because she loves her father, and she wants so much for him to see her win.

My father was fearless, while I was famously afraid of everything. At eight, I went with my friend Laura's family to a Bible conference in Montreat, North Carolina. We stayed in a huge old house on the side of a mountain. Daddy came later and slept in the basement, far away down a narrow flight of gray stairs. I stayed on the third floor, and all week it stormed like crazy. Thunder rattled the wooden house at night; rainy wind blew in our open windows. I lay awake terrified, feeling as if I'd been hung out in the wind and lightning all alone, while Daddy and the others slept.

On Friday things cleared up enough for a hike on another mountain nearby. I walked up with Laura and her brother Larry while the adults walked ahead. When we reached the top, we saw that the weather had changed once again: a cloud now hung across the blue sky like a swag of black and silver cloth. The yellow of the valley deepened; the green treetops became sharp and brilliant. Only a thin line of blue remained beneath the curtain of the sky, as if another world were closing to us and a new one opening up.

My heart began to pound. We heard a clapping noise; then the treetops bent, thunder rumbled, lightning flashed. Rain pummeled us. But Daddy was laughing. Why should he be afraid of a storm? He'd survived war, fire, wind, loss— everything I could fear in life. What was a little rain to any of that?

He picked me up and swung me out over a rock face, a cliff, probably thinking he could tease the fear out of me. I yelled, "Don't! Stop! Put me down!" I was partly afraid, partly ashamed at being so afraid. Why couldn't I be strong like him? I would never do the great things that he did. A few moments later, everyone began hurrying down the mountain to escape the lightning. I lost sight of Daddy, far behind me. I ran with Larry, who was crying and shaking. Finally he stopped and dropped to his knees.

"Larry!" I yelled. "What are you doing?"

"Praying!"

"Well, for gosh sakes, pray while you run!"

Later, at dinner, everyone laughed as I told the story. I watched Daddy's face as he looked away, chuckling and shaking his head. I wondered if he was ashamed of me: I wished I had a shadow of his courage.

Out on the Hopewell High School track, on that February morning, I ran my first half mile at my usual two minutes a lap. My chest ached from the cold, but the worst was over. I began to feel warm and loose. I kept checking my stopwatch, running against it. On the fourth lap I took a slight sprint at the end, then realized I could stop but kept going anyway. I was getting my second wind. Pretty soon I might get the happy feeling of easy speed, the sense of rising out of my own body, watching myself going around and around the asphalt loops. This was what I always waited for, the feeling that joy was automatic, that pain was a faraway dream.

I caught up to my father going at his slightly quicker pace. He usually ran a 6:30 mile. I stayed beside him and we ran together, without speaking, for another four laps. Each lap seemed a little faster. We were pushing each other on. The cold air felt good against my face. I heard his breathing but I didn't look over at him.

On the last lap, I sprang forward and ran as fast as I could. My chest burned, my legs felt weak, but I kept control of my stride. Daddy had picked up his pace even more. He ran slightly ahead of me. We came to the last hundred yards and I broke out, sprinting on my toes, not looking back. I clicked the watch as I crossed the line. Six minutes. Later, at home, through my bedroom door I heard him say to my mother, "She ran so fast today. I could barely keep up with her."

Hearing those words was like winning an Olympic medal. I don't think I ever ran as hard again as I did that morning. Daddy had let me beat him, of course; he'd moved over to let me pass. But he'd seen me at my very fastest. He'd admired my speed, and even inspired me to run faster. He'd seen *me*.

I think of the Old Testament story of Jacob on the night he wrestled a mysterious man till nearly dawn.* Before the sun rose, Jacob held the man fast and demanded a blessing. The man touched the hollow of Jacob's thigh and left him with a wound and a new name, "Israel," or "Prince with God."

"Thou hast prevailed," said the man, before he slipped away. Afterwards, Jacob called the place "Peniel," meaning "face of God." He said, "I have seen God face to face, and my life is preserved."

My father could have beaten me in our race, but he let me prevail. I like to think that he took joy in my joy, not because he thought that I'd accomplish great things one day, but because his love for me, buried under many distractions, was great. On that winter morning he was fully my Daddy: running beside me, cheering me on, racing with me side–by–side, and meeting me face-to-face. In my heart I held onto the day as a promise of things to come. It raised hopes that would sometimes be bruised, sometimes crushed, yet it gave me a picture of what love could be: the picture was ultimately worth any disappointment.

6
exile

She stood in the corner of the bride's room, wanting to say: I love the two of you so much and you are the we of me. Please take me with you from the wedding, for we belong to be together.

—Carson McCullers, *The Member of the Wedding*

Now, the word of the Lord came to Kennedy Smartt. And the Lord said, "Arise. Get thee up to Atlanta, that great city, and dwell in it; for there have I established a denomination, to be a denomination for all Presbyterians who have not yet bowed the knee to Baal."

So he gathered about him his household, his wife, and his youngest daughter, and also his car (a Vega). And they made ready to leave. And they tarried not, but arose and went to Atlanta, he and his wife and his youngest daughter, and also their car. They came to the city in the sixth month of the year and dwelt upon a great highway, ten miles from Stone Mountain.

I've always seen Christianity as a religion of exile. For much of human history, people worshiped in one holy place or another: in tabernacles and temples, on mountaintops and in sacred groves. To be religious was to do sacred things in sacred places. But Jesus taught that even the Temple of Solomon was only a symbol, and that the holy city of Jerusalem would soon pass away. *The kingdom of God is within you,** he said, and *the hour cometh . . . when the true worshipers shall worship the Father in spirit and in truth. . . .*** It was a great promise, but also a great burden. A thousand years after Jesus' death, medieval Crusaders beat their way back to Jerusalem under the emblem of the cross. If the kingdom of heaven was within them, they decided they'd like an external kingdom, too, one that could be taken by bloodshed. The thought of a physical Jerusalem stirred their hearts as much as the promise of heaven.

Most of us still long for a holy city on earth. We want a Jerusalem of our own. Like Jews wandering in the desert, like Crusaders, we imagine one place as more divine than any other—not necessarily a city or a country, but a point where heaven and earth meet and we experience the reality of God. It's not enough to talk about the joy that waits for us after death in God's immaterial kingdom, that unimaginable city of peace, where suffering and sadness disappear. We can't endure the wait! All our lives just to look forward to the consummation of our spiritual hopes? No. If not today, then tomorrow or the next day, we'll catch sight of some earthly temple, some material rest. It may be a home, a possession, a friend, a child, a lover—and we'll go there, thinking that this is it at last, the city of God in all its splendor.

In a certain way, my father's church in Virginia will always be my temple. Hopewell itself will be my holy city. When I was small and my Sunday school teachers called the church building "God's House," I imagined that God the Father literally lived in the attic. I pictured him sitting up there on a box like the Ark of the Covenant, staring out of a stained glass window at the people in the streets below. Even when I knew better, I still thought of the church as a holy place, and our town as a holy land. It didn't look all that holy, but it was the city of my father, the city where I myself had been born. All my early revelations—about my helplessness before God, about death, about love—had come to me there. I imagined God sitting square in the middle of everything.

And then, when I was twelve years old, a "call" suddenly came upon my father. It was the spirit of exodus. He told us that he planned to leave the pastorate and take up a peripatetic sort of ministry for our new denomination. We would move to Atlanta. He would become a traveling preacher, speaking out of town every weekend except Christmas. My sister was staying in Virginia for the summer and then heading off to college. Mama and I would be the only ones left at home.

At the outset, I really didn't mind moving. It seemed like a welcome distraction from puberty, or rather my lack of it. The girls I'd grown up with were wearing makeup and getting their hair sculpted into feathery helmets. I was tiny and flat-chested, with square, gold-frame glasses that Daddy insisted I get because they'd be "sturdier for sports." One day I wore a training bra to school, just for the sake of feeling like everybody else. I didn't think anyone would notice, but a girl in the lunch line screeched and plucked at the strap on my shoulder.

"My gosh, do *you* have a bra on?"

"No!" I said. "It's a . . . a bandage."

"A bandage? For what?"

"For my broken collar bone!"

Obviously, adolescence wasn't going well, and I thought it might go better somewhere else. To a certain extent, that was foolish. I couldn't shed my body, after all. Yet I sensed rightly that in moving I'd leave a lot of myself behind. What a hope! No longer to be the pastor's daughter, the tomboy, the football and karate freak. I'd have a chance to start over, separated from all the stuff that had defined me.

Everything that happened to me in Virginia now seems like a myth: part history and part fantasy. From photographs and various documents in the bottom drawer of my sewing machine cabinet, I can prove that I lived there. I have a birth certificate from Hopewell Hospital. I have report cards and yearbooks from West End Christian School and pictures of Laura and me at Monticello. My real history, though, begins on the day we moved to Atlanta. My sister graduated from high school on a Friday night. On Saturday morning we told her good-bye. Then Mama, Daddy, and I drove from Southern Virginia to North Georgia, weaving down through the Carolinas, sometimes discussing what our new home would be like. My parents had a better idea of it than I did. They had spent several years in Georgia in the late 1950s: first while Daddy attended Columbia Seminary in Decatur, and then while he was pastoring Ingleside Presbyterian in Scottdale. Atlanta hadn't reached so far out in those days. The land around Decatur had remained rural and pretty, though poor.

"So will we go to Ingleside Presbyterian now?" I asked.

"No," my mother said.

"Why not? Is it a bad church?"

"Oh, my, no!" She looked shocked. "We still have wonderful friends at Ingleside. But Daddy works for the new denomination now."

"Then what church are we going to?"

"Good church," said Daddy. "Preacher's a fine man. Went to Reformed Seminary in Jackson, Mississippi."

"And he used to be a dancer," said Mama. "Right, Ken? He and his wife were both dancers."

"*Ballet* dancers," said Daddy.

"I think ballet is beautiful," said my mother.

"If you like that sort of thing," said Daddy.

I tried to process this information: the fact that a fine pastor who'd attended Reformed Seminary in Jackson, Mississippi, had once been a *ballet dancer*. I tried to imagine my own fine pastor-father dancing ballet and couldn't. I had no category in my mind for preachers who danced at all.

It took us ten hours to reach Atlanta. I woke up from a nap and saw that we were traveling on a wide, busy highway. Pine trees towered over parking lots on both sides of the road. The sky was hot and blue above us. Down a big hill and up another, we turned right and drove into our new neighborhood. This was it. Our house-to-be sat halfway down a hill, at the bottom of a steep driveway.

"It'll be so hard to get out of here if there's ice," said Mama, as we parked. "Ken, we didn't think about ice. How will we get out of this driveway if there's ice?"

"We shall cross that bridge when we come to it," said Daddy cheerfully, and he hopped out and fetched our suitcases while Mama gathered up the trash in the car. For the first time, we had an automatic garage door. Daddy handed me the small plastic box and I pressed the button ceremoniously. Vruummmm . . . The wide door opened with a huge, rushing squeak, like the cry of an injured whale. And then we invaded. I followed my father into the garage and through a dark doorway, over the threshold into our new house.

"Welcome home," Daddy said.

I nodded and walked back alone, through a wide, empty room with a big glass door that opened onto a second-storey deck. Skinny dogwoods hung over the deck rail, framing a sky full of deep green leaves. I kept going back to the room they'd picked to be mine. It was all done in black and white, with shag carpet and newsprint walls. A red sticker stuck on a wall outlet said, "Love!"

I could hear Mama's voice down the hall. "I smell a dog," she said. "Ken, do you smell a dog?" After a few minutes she came into my room and turned a crank on my new aluminum frame window, which suddenly cracked into three parts. "Oh, my, the smell. I wonder if it was one dog or were there more?"

"I can't smell anything," I said. "Did hippies live in here?"

I pointed at the Love! sticker and she glanced at it. "Well, I wouldn't think so. The owners didn't seem like hippies when I met them. But it is strange. Why would anyone want such gloomy black curtains?"

"I like black curtains," I said, remembering that my sister had once wanted to paint our room black: I'd hated the idea at the time, preferring pink or blue. But now, with adolescence upon me, I favored the gloomy colors. I looked out onto the front yard and thought that the pine trees on our new lawn looked like telephone poles. Their branches started so high above the house that you couldn't see them from the window.

That same day we began to unpack our stuff, and soon we had recreated the Hopewell house inside this one: same dark dining room furniture, same piano and brass clock with wide leaf border, same sofa, same TV with four channels, same bookcases and books and brick red recliner and mustard yellow ottoman. On Sunday, I woke up in my black-and-white bedroom and took a shower in my new bathroom, which had two sinks and pink wallpaper decorated with swirling silver clouds. I put on my best dress. Then we drove to our new church in the small city of Stone Mountain, with Daddy clocking the trip on the odometer.

"It's exactly seven miles from our house to the church," he announced, as we pulled into the gravel parking lot of a tiny white building with a sign out front that said "Grace Presbyterian Church. Reformed, Evangelical." Daddy searched for a parking place under a stand of oak trees, on the other side of sheltered picnic tables. We got out of the car and walked up the sagging steps to the porch of the church. On our left was a door that said, "Gentlemen." A man handed us a bulletin and we went in.

The building looked about a hundred years old. Church members had whitewashed the walls, cleaned the floors, and decorated the windows with contact paper of a generic stained-glass design. None of these beautification efforts had quite worked, but the windows were open, and from out-doors came the summer scent of oak trees and grass. A young man played the prelude to worship on an out-of-tune upright piano: *Praise to the Lord, the Almighty, the King of Creation.**** Mama looked nervous. Daddy was on his feet, introducing himself to everyone around. He seemed to know half the congregation already.

"I'm Kennedy Smartt. And what was your name? Well, yes, I remember you! I met you in Asheville in the summer of '72. Tell me, how is your mother. . . ?"

"That lady there is the pastor's wife," Mama whispered to me as a pretty woman with smooth black hair and brown skin came toward us. The woman smiled brightly, but passed by and knocked on a door to our left. I looked up at her and then back at my mother. Two pastors' wives couldn't have been more different: Mama with her modest clothes, a cameo pinned chastely at her neck; and this lady with heavy, overdrawn eye shadow and wide, white teeth. The door opened and we heard a baby squall as she went in. I felt she should have stopped and spoken to us. Mama licked her lips and fumbled with her bulletin.

The off-key piano music stopped. The pastor himself rose to the pulpit and the service commenced, including announcements, the usual three or four hymns, the taking of tithes and offerings, an interminable prayer, and a sermon that seemed three hours long. I looked at my father, who sat beside us with his chin thrust out. As far back as I could remember, I'd never sat next to him in church on a Sunday morning. The sight of him in profile was a bit of a shock. Where'd he get that scar? And what was he thinking about all this time? Was he listening? Could he really sit quiet and still for so long?

As for the new minister, I was disappointed he wasn't wearing a ballet costume. I'd expected him to preach in black tights and Danskins. Instead he wore a black robe with dusty wingtips showing underneath. His speaking style was slow, careful, untheatrical. He offered no jokes, no props, no moving stories of true-life drama. Never would he have told the one about the boy stuck in the bridge gears and the father who chose to save five hundred strangers on the train. Never would he have told about the woman running into the burning building to save her baby. He did have the entertaining habit of pointing down at the Bible with his middle finger. Round about his second point, a long-haired girl got up and went into a room marked "Ladies" just to the right of the pulpit. Her thick-heeled shoes sounded like horse hooves on the wood floor. We heard a loud flush as he reached his third point, and then the girl emerged from the bathroom and took her seat again before the preacher began his long approach to the benediction.

Then I thought, *Here I am in my Sunday dress with my Bible on my lap and they say this is church, but I'm sitting on a metal folding chair rather than a pew, and in a small crowd of strangers rather than among hundreds of good friends, and I'm listening to a man in priest clothes instead of my own father in a blue suit tossing out jokes and stories.* Church was supposed to be a great, tall-steepled, many-roomed building with holy places hidden in its nooks and crannies. It was the place where I had always been the youngest daughter, the darling, the center of everything.

I felt like a dog dropped off at a kennel. I felt homeless.

Atlanta seemed unbearably hot that first summer, even hotter than Hopewell, which had always been plenty steamy. A mile from our house sat Columbia Square Mall, an aging shopping center that had two department stores, lots of little shops, and a Baskin Robbins. Often I asked Mama if I could walk up there and get ice cream.

"Let's pin your key to your underwear," Mama said. Her biggest worry was that I'd find myself locked out if she ran an errand. I dutifully pinned the garage key to the elastic band of my panties and then walked down our quiet street, squinting in the thick sunlight. I took a shortcut behind Avondale High School stadium and stopped in to visit the stadium itself, which was set on a hill above the neighborhood. I only had to walk through a tunnel and suddenly I was high up in the air, looking out over the terraced concrete steps, the empty football field, the side street dipping into the neighborhood below. Everything seemed quiet and empty. The tall pine trees were like green clouds swirling above the charcoal-colored roofs of the houses. Leaving the stadium, I stepped across a square of pavement someone had written on long ago.

"What is Reality?"

I laughed at the question, which seemed so dated. It was a relic from my oldest brother's era—the late 1960s when ordinary people went around asking profound philosophical questions. Nowadays people concentrated on immediate, material perplexities, such as "How much does gas cost?" But of course, in my heart I was asking this same question. What *is* real?

Was I real even though I'd left behind everything I'd started out with? The last few years had been a gradual peeling away of the outer layers that defined me. I'd given up a brother, then another brother, then my grandmother, and now, this very summer, our house and town and church and even my sister, who had started to become a friend. Mama was no longer a preacher's wife, and I was no longer the daughter of a locally famous man. We were people in exile, cast down from our former glory, wandering in the wilderness. Would we wander forever?

For someone who becomes a Christian later in life, maybe it really is easy to believe that God goes *with* you. You accept that he's been watching you all along, and so you naturally assume his presence. You don't have to be in Jerusalem. You know that you can speak to God or worship anywhere—in a garden, in a desert, in a small town, in a big city—because you, as the temple of the Holy Spirit, carry the Holy of Holies in your own heart.

But when you've grown up in Jerusalem itself, when you've put a floor and ceiling and walls to your faith, to step outside those walls can be like going into exile, leaving the city behind. Outside the walls, you take one last look at what can never be recovered. Then you turn and gaze ahead, asking yourself what remains. "Who am I now? Where is this? Is home gone forever?"

Of course, there are certain freedoms that come with exile. At the mall, after drinking a root beer purchased for twenty-five cents from the Sears cafeteria, I looked at records and then went to the paperback shelves and rifled through book after book. This was not an encounter with great literature. I'd discovered that the wells of sin ran deep in the middle of Sears and Roebuck. Oh, the hours I spent there, week after week that summer, reading Jacqueline Susann, Harold Robbins, Judith Krantz. With my key still pinned to my underwear, I absorbed it all with the greatest pleasure and yearning for more: things carnal, things worldly, things incomprehensible. Meanwhile, people came and went past me in the aisles, but I didn't care. So what if strangers saw that I was reading trash? I didn't know them. I was nobody here: I was barely real. I turned toward home after getting a hot fudge sundae; "I'm all alone," I thought, with great pleasure. "No one can stop me from doing anything I want." I wondered what else I could do without anybody finding out about it.

One morning in August I walked up to the mall, bought a pack of Marlboros from a restaurant machine, and smoked half of them in the sprawling blue bathroom of Davidson's Department Store, with rows and rows of empty stalls on either side of me. For half an hour, the only noise in the room was the occasional snap of my match striking. Finally, I changed into new clothes from a sack I'd brought with me, pushed the old clothes into the white metal trashcan along with the leftover cigarettes, and walked home.

I'd been raised to think of smoking as rebellion against a holy God, the shaking of an unfiltered, unmentholated fist at heaven. But I felt no guilt about it, any more than I did about reading dirty books. I had no sense that God was looking over my shoulder, because God, after all, did not live around here. He was back in Hopewell. What I did feel bad about was lying to my mother, which I'd rarely done before. My mother, once so close, so protecting, so strong—I now saw her as a victim of my new worldliness.

"What have you been doing at the mall?" she'd say, and I'd say, "Looking around," in a dismissive voice. I raged first at myself for being deceptive, then at her for being so gullible. She should know me better than this. She should see through me.

Then I began to see how lonely she was in our new city, pushed to the periphery as my father began his travels, and I felt compassion for her. I loved my mother more than anyone. I wanted her to be important again. I wanted our life to be as it had been—or at least as I had perceived it, with my Daddy at the center of the church and her next to him, and everything else, no matter how distant, revolving around the two of them. I wanted to tell Mama all of these things I'd done and felt, but I was afraid of the harm I might do. I imagined her staring at me with frail, quizzical sadness, like a suffering animal: "How could you be such an ungrateful daughter? How could you disappoint me this way?"

So I kept quiet, and protected her from my dangerous thirteen-year-old self. "What are you thinking about?" she asked me one night as we drove quietly through the dark on the way to prayer meeting. "Why are you so quiet? Why don't you talk to me like you used to?"

"I don't know," I said. "No reason."

A few weeks before I started the eighth grade, I played piano for Vacation Bible School at our little schoolhouse church. Nobody seemed to care that I wasn't much good at it. My hands shook whenever I had to play a chord with more than two notes. At the closing ceremonies, the lady in charge went down the list of helpers thanking everyone, but forgot about me. Since I was so new, I didn't feel hurt. I figured she hadn't learned my name.

But the preacher's wife got up and made a special announcement: "I think we ought to be sure and thank our pianist, Betty, because she did a great job and put so much time into this."

Everyone turned and clapped for me enthusiastically—embarrassed to have forgotten, maybe. I looked around, amazed. After church I sought out the preacher's wife. She was on the porch of the church, squinting in the sun, with her youngest child on her hip.

"Thank you," I said.

She was barely taller than I was. She looked me straight in the eye and gave me a beautiful, bright smile, like a white bird lifting its wings. "You're welcome."

"Is it true you were a ballerina?" I asked.

She nodded. "Why don't you come visit us one afternoon? I have a piano. I'd love for someone to play it."

It was a simple thing for her to say. She invited all kinds of people over, as I found out later. So how can I explain that she became, at that moment, my own Jerusalem? I see the two of us facing each other on those porch steps on an August day: we met as two halves of a whole, a map ripped in half and rejoined. I was a child with parents who loved me, and yet I was an orphan and an exile. She stood at the center of our church, smiling at me with a baby in her arms, the very archetype of home.

It was as if she pointed at some temple behind us, beckoning me to a secret Holy of Holies. "Come with me!" her eyes said. "Come with me, and all will be as it was!"

7

a telltale heart

But, alas, what avails the vigilance against the destiny of man? Not even these well-contrived securities sufficed to save, from the uttermost agonies of living inhumation, a wretch to these agonies foredoomed!

—Edgar Allan Poe, "The Premature Burial"

So, thinking of myself as an exile, unable to wait for God to come close, I left behind the spiritual fervor of my childhood. I dropped Jesus like a hot coal and turned away, looking for someone easier to hang onto. I no longer dreamed about doing heroic things for God—sacrificing myself, hanging on some public cross. I didn't ask God to show me miracles or let me speak in tongues. I didn't care about witnessing or winning souls. The little girl who had written "Trust in the Lord with All Thy Heart and Lean Not on Thine Own Understanding" on sidewalks in Virginia disappeared, and in her place stood a young cynic.

My new passion was ridicule: identifying the idiotic and improbable. As a young teenager, I naturally tried to protect myself from looking ridiculous, and at the same time identify the ridiculous in everyone else. I wasn't so good at the first part, but very talented at the second. I ridiculed the tall-haired deacon who sang an off-key version of "Chestnuts Roasting on an Open Fire" at a Christmas service. I laughed at the Sunday school teacher who told us that the sign above the cross was written in Roman, Jewish, and Hebrew. I imitated the old lady with the fluttery eyelids and overdrawn lipstick who never listened to anything people told her but went around saying to everyone, "Itn't that wunderful!" I'd forgotten, I guess, the Bible story about wild bears gobbling up little boys after they made fun of the prophet Elisha (2 Kings 2:23–24).

But while I lost my passion for God, and while I became so disparaging about most people, my need for a few people only grew and grew. My love for the preacher's wife belied all my cynicism. She was, to me, the physical point where heaven and earth meet. If Soviet soldiers had asked me to spit on her picture, I'd have taken a bullet, gladly. I'd have sacrificed myself without a second thought.

Our church, though we had a building plan, still met in the schoolhouse. Sometimes it seemed little more than a tent: big rains lashed the roof so hard we couldn't hear the preacher. Wind made the walls creak. Frost crackled over the windows and snuck under the door, chilling everybody to the bone. On cold Sunday nights, I'd sit by the preacher's wife: she'd put her arm around the back of my chair, and

during long prayers I'd lay my head against the crook of her
elbow, like any six-year-old girl—only, I was thirteen. I knew
I looked babyish and silly, but once again I had a strong
feeling that, when I was close to this particular woman, I
gained back all that was lost. So what if I looked foolish?

On Thursday nights, she took me with her to an adult
ballet class that she taught in northeast Atlanta. It was a long
drive and it was my favorite time of the week. We talked
all the way, discussing everything from Presbyterian doctrine
to the ups and downs of her sex life. Because of her openness
with me, I felt not childish now but extraordinarily preco-
cious—womanly, even. I impressed her with the way I could
carry my own in a conversation, scattering out adult words
like a pigeon walking through birdseed.

"You," she'd say again and again, "are so mature for your
age. Are you sure you're not a midget?"

"I'm damned sure," I said.

"You seem like a thirty-year-old in disguise."

It was gratifying to be told I was mature. To my way of
thinking, my brothers and sister treated me like I actually
was *six years old*, even when I behaved in a thoroughly adult
manner. They laughed at none of my witty comments, they
pointed out that my hair needed work and my eyeglasses
made me look like a skinny insect. With them, I'd be forever
prepubescent. But the preacher's wife said I acted like a thirty-
year-old. She let me in on visits with adult friends, she took

me shopping with her, and to ballet, and even on vacation. How could I not adore her? Without her, I was an awkward seventh grader, but with her, I was a maturing young woman. She gave me a vision of myself as poised and developed, someone who could hold my own.

"*You* are the very best friend I will ever have," I told her once.

"And you're my best friend, too," she said, warmly. "I love you like a daughter."

My own mother was always kind and respectful to the preacher's wife. Their natural sympathy for each other surprised me, since in most obvious ways, they were opposites. Mama had a godly and serious nature—too serious for her to make friends easily. She didn't like small talk. She was fiercely honest. She worried all the time about expressing her opinions too boldly in church meetings. The preacher's wife, on the other hand, was theatrical and irreverent. Some people wished her husband would rein her in, but it was hard to imagine how he'd do it. With chains? A cat-o'-nine-tails? Her free manner shocked some of the good church ladies.

"She's teaching me ballet in exchange for babysitting," I told one woman, who'd asked in a suspicious voice why we spent so much time together.

"*Really?*" the woman smirked. "And what *else* is she teaching you?"

My mother, though, defended the preacher's wife to her critics. I'd always seen Mama as the very holiest woman on earth; now I saw that she was compassionate, too, and, in her way, open-minded. She'd experienced much loneliness in her twenty-five years of ministry with my father. She knew how it felt to struggle before a congregation of Christians, to be hungry for fellowship and love in the place where most people go to find those very things. Still, she worried about me spending days at a time with someone so much older. She expressed it in a roundabout way at first, saying things like, "Betty, does she smoke? I smell cigarettes on her sometimes."

"Yes, Mama."

"Does she smoke in the car with you?"

"Sometimes."

"I hope you would never smoke."

"Oh no, Mama. I don't want cancer."

At other times, Mama focused her worry on ballet and my increasing love of the theater. I'd been making up plays since I was little, performing them at school or for friends. I was now too old to hope for a career as a ballerina, but I dreamed of dancing on Broadway one day. My idol was Barbra Streisand: like her, I wanted to act onstage and in movies and maybe even sing. Mama heard me belting out tunes from *Funny Girl* in the bathtub. She saw me heading off to school in theatrical clothes, climbing onto my bicycle some mornings in white go-go boots and a leopard-skin vest.

"Don't you have *any* desire to be like the other girls?" she said.

"Other girls are boring. I want to be like Barbra."

In the spring, a friend at school told me they were auditioning kids for a play at the Alliance Theater downtown. I talked to my mother in the kitchen one night and begged her to take me into Atlanta for the audition.

"And what would you do when you got up in front of those people to audition?"

"I don't know. I haven't thought of anything yet."

She shook her head and sat down at the kitchen table. "Do you know," she said, "that I used to like drama myself? Once, back when I was teaching school in New Jersey, I recited the beginning of 'The Telltale Heart' in a student production. They said I was very good."

"Really?" I was astounded to hear this. After all her protests about the worldliness of the theater.

"Yes."

"Can you remember any of it?"

She paused and demonstrated the first few lines, rubbing her hands together anxiously. *True! Nervous—very nervous, dreadfully nervous I had been and am.* * She stopped and laughed. "I must sound pretty funny."

"I think you sound good!" I looked at my mother, maybe for the first time appreciating that there were things about her I didn't understand, couldn't guess. I went back to my room and considered a little longer. Finally I retrieved *Edgar Allen Poe Stories* from the living room bookshelf and read through the first page of "The Telltale Heart." It certainly was a dramatic piece. I had planned to do comedy, but the range of emotion that this called for would undoubtedly impress a director. Could I handle it? Could I be convincing? I read the first few lines out loud, then stood up and began reading with real feeling.

Over the next few days I practiced and practiced the part aloud, trying to become at ease with the character. Mama helped me memorize my lines: she sat at the kitchen table with sewing pins between her lips, glancing over at the text, and nodding at me. "Mmm-hmmm . . ." Meanwhile, the preacher's wife had become very busy lately. I saw her only once, but I had enough time to beg her to go with us to the audition and recommend me to the theater director.

She laughed. "He wouldn't know me."

"But he may have seen you dance once. You were in *West Side Story*."

"I was a dancer in the chorus line."

"You were a professional," I said. "That's something. At least write me a letter of reference."

She wrote me a note in ballpoint pen, addressed to "Whom It May Concern."

I would like to recommend Betty Smartt for a part in your play. Betty is a good ballet student and has a lot of dedication. I also think that she has the potential to be a fine actress.

Yours, &&,

On the day of the audition Mama drove me downtown and went to lunch while I stood in line in the theater lobby, waiting my turn. After about forty-five minutes, they called me up. I walked onto the stage in a blue sundress and sandals, my straight hair flopping over the rims of my glasses and my braces glinting in the lights. I held my letter from the preacher's wife in my hand.

"Should I give this to someone?" I said.

"What is it?"

"A letter of reference."

"Leave it on the stage."

"OK." I couldn't make out any faces, just three heads lined up in a distant row. I dragged a metal chair to center stage, then sat down and leaned forward. I cleared my throat and began.

True! Nervous—very nervous, dreadfully nervous I had been and am. But why will you say that I am mad?

I got up from the chair and walked around it as I spoke.

*How then am I mad? Hearken, and observe how healthily, how calmly I can tell you the whole story. . . .***

I kept going, thinking I would never get to the end of the piece. My voice was lost in the hugeness of the place. At last I finished and stood with my hands on the back of the chair.

"Thank you," said one of the men out there. "We'll call you by this weekend if we need you."

"OK," I said. "Don't forget my references."

I left the letter and trudged offstage, back into the lobby. My mother was outside on the steps, standing in the sunshine. I squinted at her in the glare.

"Were you nervous?" she asked.

"Yes. Very nervous."

"How did you do?"

"I don't know. I don't think very well."

"Well," she said in a comforting voice, "I think it's wonderful that you tried."

By the end of the weekend, nobody had called from the theater. On Sunday afternoon I walked around anxiously, skipped church (pretending to be sick), and then went to bed still expecting the phone to ring. I didn't fall asleep till well after midnight.

Of course, the phone didn't ring. The next day I moped around sadly. I went over my lines again, rehearsing my imperfections. How ridiculous I must have looked! Like Andrea McCardle playing Lady Macbeth. I continued to wander aimlessly for the following several days, feeling gloomy, wishing for comfort.

"I think you should pray that God will bring something new into your life," Mama said gently. "Maybe a new interest besides the theater."

"I don't need a new interest!" What was wrong with my mother that she couldn't see this? The preacher's wife would understand, even if Mama didn't. But I couldn't seem to get hold of the preacher's wife. I called again and again, dialing her number many times a day on the black phone in my parents' bedroom. She was always either too busy to talk, or not at home.

"She's out with a friend," her husband would say, or "I'm not sure where she is," or "I think she's gone shopping with somebody."

The following week, she left a message at my house that she couldn't take me to ballet on Thursday night. When I approached her at church, I found her distracted with her children, then in a conversation with adult friends, then busy in the kitchen, and then simply gone. I tried to speak to her the next week, too, but she was always occupied, always too busy to talk. I felt like a small child waiting to be noticed, wishing for attention.

One Sunday night, on the way home from church, Mama asked me what was wrong. "You're very quiet tonight," she said. "Has something upset you?"

Her voice was so kind that I couldn't hold back tears. The truth rushed out of me. I began to tell her everything I'd been feeling—all about my disappointment over the audition, my hurt over how the minister's wife had pulled away from me.

"Betty," Mama said softly, "I think she has too much influence over you, anyway. I think it would be better for you to find a friend your own age."

I felt betrayed. "But she's my best friend," I said. "I love her more than almost anybody!"

Mama shook her head. "You get so taken up with one thing after another. I'm worried that you'll be led into a worldly life if you're not careful. I don't want you to be guided by worldly people. I want you to be interested in the things God has for you."

I sat in the dark of the car, quietly crying as headlights streaked past us. I tried to think of a cynical answer: *And what, exactly, does God have for me? The mission field? BORneo?*

Before I formed the words, though, my mother lowered the boom. "Also," she said, "I've noticed how you act towards *her*. You treat her the way most girls treat boys."

The lights on the road went blurry. I felt myself go hot from foot to toe. In the coldest voice I could manage, I hissed an answer back at her. I've forgotten exactly what I said, but it was something vicious that left Mama silent with hurt.

It's taken me a long time to understand the relationship between my all-consuming affection for one woman and my cynicism toward the rest of the world, including my own mother. Affection and cynicism, while they seem opposed to each other, grow and move in dangerous symbiosis. Love for the preacher's wife was my most tender spot; cynicism was the armor that protected it from all threats, even my mother's threatening concern. But the words Mama spoke that night stayed with me. I thought of them many times in the years ahead. They were arrows of love, neither completely on nor off the mark.

8
beauty

He turneth a wilderness into a standing water,
and dry ground into water springs.
And there he maketh the hungry to dwell. . . .
　　　　　　　　　　　—Psalm 107:35–36a

I didn't have my ear out for God in those days, but did he ever speak to me, anyway? As I moved further and further away, did he give me an audible word, send me a dream, or show me a miracle? When I was in my mid-twenties, a friend told me that we gain faith in God through the exercise of reason rather than looking for supernatural evidence. Instead of hoping for miracles and visions, we ought to seek God in prayer and obedience to the Scriptures—that is, in dutiful, passionless Christianity.

At the time, I accepted my friend's rational approach to religion because I didn't see any other approach possible. It made no sense to hope for miracles that I knew wouldn't come. To want them and not get them was worse than not to want them at all.

As a young child, though, I'd hoped for miracles every day and expected them to happen, prayed for them to happen, never considered for a moment that they wouldn't happen. My mother's prayers and our readings in the Gospels had taught me to look for spiritual realities behind the curtain of our material existence. I believed wholeheartedly in the presence of things I couldn't see: angels and demons hovering in corners, fluttering through hallways. I chalked up much of what I *could* see (but couldn't understand) to mystery: telephones, pianos, newborn babies. These were all miracles to me as a child, and in my mind there was no clear line between the world of sense and the world of spirit.

Moving out of childhood, I watched that world of spirit shrink: every day brought a new diminishment of mystery, until most things became predictable and dull. The loss fed my natural cynicism. It made me doubt that anything existed beyond what we could perceive through a combination of our physical senses and technology. Yet even as a cynical teenager, I had a shred left of my childish faith. I sometimes prayed "God, show me that you're real," though I wasn't sure anybody listened. If God existed, maybe he revealed himself only in his own time, on rare occasions. After all, Moses hadn't been seeking a flaming bush; Samuel hadn't listened for God in the dark of the night; the prophet Ezekiel hadn't asked for a vision of the Lord in captivity:

> *And I looked, and, behold, a whirlwind came out of the north, a great cloud, and a fire enfolding itself, and a*

brightness was about it. . . . And above the firmament . . .
was the likeness of a throne, as the appearance of a sapphire
stone; and upon the likeness of the throne was the likeness as
the appearance of a man above upon it. . . . *

I envied Ezekiel that vision. I thought that if I had a
beautiful vision like his, I'd never doubt God again. Once,
waking up from a dream, I thought I felt something lying on
my chest, choking me—an invisible, evil presence like heavy
hands around my throat. I said the Twenty-third Psalm aloud
and felt the pressure ease, my fear ebb away—but only a few
seconds later I doubted the whole experience. I wished I
could prove to myself that something had really pressed me
down in the dark, and that I hadn't been (as seemed more
likely) stuck in the tail end of a nightmare. Another time I
prayed, "If you're there, God, make an angel appear before me!"
I clenched my teeth and squinted, half wishing, half dreading
that a thunderbolt would rip through the veil of night and reveal
seraphim glowing on the windowsill. Nothing happened: I saw
no seraphim, only the streetlights shining through my window
on my wall. Eventually I decided that I never would see anything
surprising; angels (even if they existed, and I wasn't sure)
didn't appear to young girls on command. Prayer never
brought about the great miracles I'd once believed in.

In some ways, the theology of our church made it easy
for a cynical teenager to lose her faith gradually, almost

imperceptibly. Not that there isn't much good in Presbyterianism and in Reformed theology. Reformed Presbyterians emphasize the grace of God, which offers freedom from guilt and moral obligation. They teach that Christians don't need to work their way into God's favor, because Christ has released us from the wrath of heaven and brought us directly into the presence of the Divine. We are set free to obey God.

Yet in the confidence of that freedom, it's easy to sacrifice a longing to see God at work in the world now—an urge to see his power and beauty impinge upon the material. At my childhood churches, we lived very much in the ordinary, expecting next to nothing in the way of the supernatural. In worship we had no holy water, no incense, no confessional, no vestments. We didn't consider Christ to be truly present in the elements of the Lord's Supper. We didn't claim to speak the language of the Spirit: most of us didn't even like to pray aloud in English.

Our worship services were straightforward affairs. We sat dutifully, holding Bibles on our laps. We stared at our bulletins and then at the faces of the people up front who talked a lot because that's what tradition demanded of them, even on days when they had little to say. At the end of our worship the deacons brought up the plates and stood at the Remembrance table, barely moving their lips with us while we sang, "Praise God from Whom all Blessings Flow." Most

Sundays, we were very orderly people. We could have been the audience at the taping of a Bill Moyers special.

All in all, we held to the convictions my friend expressed when she said that faith is a matter of reason—of thinking things out correctly. While admitting that the Holy Spirit must direct our reason, we'd inherited a conviction that God's direction will reveal itself in seemliness and orderliness. But is it possible to worship a Being who is unspeakably beautiful, ineffably strange—the God who appeared to Ezekiel—and never do anything *surprising?* Never even be *surprised?*

It's fine to say, as my rational friend would, that God speaks to our hearts through Scripture and prayer and, yes, even those epic Reformed sermons. But can we ever expect anything else? When we're shipwrecked in the ordinary, when we've lost our hope in miracles and even in the reality of God, will God himself intervene, step into our intellectual religion, and give us something miraculous to hold to— something extraordinary, but something that touches our ordinary senses?

My life, now that I was starting high school, was in transition. I still grieved over the loss of my best friend, but I was changing and maturing quickly. Every day felt like a huge leap away from the past. Things that had happened a short time ago seemed far behind me.

At a camp in Tennessee, I got to know three slightly older girls from my own church. They were bright and artistic and funny, and I wanted to be one of them: to share in their interests, their jokes, their treasury of made-up epithets for people they didn't like (kinsnerdees, poindexters, Velveeta Cheesers). I slipped into my usual role of worshiper and acolyte, and before long, I'd become a sort of mascot to their discriminating society. While hiking in the Smoky Mountains, we talked about poetry; we argued over theology and sang hymns in three-part harmony. We made up our own silly rounds by combining unlikely songs, such as the theme to a popular Japanese cartoon with "Go Tell Aunt Rhody" and "Out of the Ivory Palaces." Good conversation is better to me than good food. I was so happy and satisfied in their company that I lost five pounds before I got home from camp.

One Saturday night back in Atlanta, my friends and I had a sleepover and stayed awake for hours talking about God and aesthetics. I was just fourteen and philosophy was still above my head, but I listened as the older girls discussed whether an absolute standard of beauty existed in the world. Could we agree that the music of Bach was greater than the music of, say, Dan Fogleberg (duh), or could we only agree that most people *considered* Bach's music greater?

"What is beauty, really?" they asked each other. "Is there an absolute measure of it or do we all create our own, equally valid standards?" One of the girls said that people and cultures will disagree about what's beautiful, what's tasteful. To her this proved that beauty was a relative idea, varying from person to person. Another girl said that, since God exists as a real Person, one standard of beauty could and maybe even did exist, based on God's own preference. There could be a most perfect smell, a most perfect song, a most perfect rose. Though we would never encounter it in the world, we knew that all others could be measured against it.

A perfect rose. The imagination of God. The girl who argued for absolute beauty talked about Charles Williams's novel *The Place of the Lion*, in which heavenly ideals appear on earth and swallow up their inferior copies. Lying in the dark in my sleeping bag, I felt a chill up the back of my head. It was as though I'd heard one beautiful chord: the most satisfying sound that could be imagined. It echoed in my mind each time I considered this idea: God's thoughts becoming realities, swallowing up their lesser manifestations. As I thought about it, I felt my sides ache with pleasure. In my childhood I had seen God as protector, as savior, as father, as giver of rest— someone to be longed for and looked for. But I had never seen him so clearly as a creator of joy and ecstasies, who decorated the world with continuous, perhaps even living beauties.

Before I started the ninth grade, my brother Danny came home to live with us while he worked on his doctoral degree at Emory University. This relationship promised to be yet another unequal one, with me worshiping him and taking up his gifts and interests as my own. Whether I could take up Danny's interests remained to be seen. He was what my father called "the egghead" of the family. We were all at least somewhat artistic: my mother sang and played the piano; my father painted; my brother Matt was a professional artist and a good musician—probably the most talented one of us; my sister Ellen could have been a writer: her letters were so funny that you read them again and again, laughing harder every time. But Danny was unique. Everything he tried came easily to him: car repair, macramé, medieval French, choral direction, cooking, painting, and even plumbing. He claimed he never read anything unless forced to, but he seemed to me to know everything. He'd drunk deeply from the fount of knowledge, and he'd occasionally tried to push my head under the same fount, though with limited success. For instance, he gave me the poems of John Milton when I was in the fifth grade, and I swear I tried to read them. The problem was that my education till that point hadn't prepared me for lines like,

> *Hence, loathed Melancholy,*
> *of Cerberus and blackest midnight born . . .*[**]

For reading material, I truly preferred *Spider Man* and *The Fantastic Four*. However, I enjoyed Danny's more age-appropriate gifts. From Wheaton he sent me *Bullfinch's Mythology*. I made it all the way through the book and learned lots of useful information, such as that Oceanus and Tethys are Titans who rule over the watery elements and that rich Sutras sometimes employ poor Brahmans for menial labor. Danny had always been my greatest patron in the family: now he was coming home to stay. I looked forward to it like the second coming of Christ.

Our beginning wasn't auspicious. He arrived late one night, very tired after a long plane ride. The next day he didn't appear until after lunch, and then showed us pictures from his trip to Europe. Everybody hates looking at other people's trip pictures though nobody seems to know this about anybody else. For my brother's sake, I pretended to be fascinated. For the next several days I followed him around the house, trying to act like I wasn't following. Soon he was pulling out favorite records and I was listening to Aram Khachaturian's *Gayaneh Suite*, Mussorgsky's *Pictures at an Exhibition*, Carl Orff's *Carmina Burana*.

Though as usual I was pursuing things for the sake of a person I loved, this was a glimpse of aesthetic joys greater, deeper than any I'd known so far. I began to put my life in order accordingly. I tossed aside *The Chocolate War* and asked Danny for book recommendations. *The Grapes of Wrath*, perhaps? No! Steinbeck was an idiot. Sherwood Anderson was good, he said, so I read *Winesburg, Ohio*. Salinger was OK. But Faulkner—he was king, the greatest ever. Danny recommended *As I Lay Dying*. I read it dutifully over one week during my lunch break at school. I liked the words, but I didn't understand half of what I took in. I sat in ninth-grade English trying to figure out the symbolism. What did it mean: "My Mother is a fish?"

I had begun Latin in the eighth grade. Now, at Danny's prompting, I added French. I had a good teacher, but it was my brother who pushed me forward. We studied together at night, taking turns reading from one of his old books: a small, battered 1905 edition of *Contes de Fees: Classic Fairy Tales for Beginners in French*. We began with "Le Petit Chaperon Rouge" ("Little Red Riding Hood") and went on to "La Barbe Bleue" ("Blue Beard"). I simultaneously loved and hated these sessions. I loved the attention and companionship: sitting in our dark family room with him at night while the clock ticked past 11:30, my mother long since gone to bed. I loved the sound of the French words, and I was thrilled when I translated a hard passage and Danny praised me. But the hard work exhausted me. Some nights I longed to stop, yet I didn't know how to ask him to stop, because I was afraid he'd stop altogether.

One day, when my brother was out, I went downstairs to find myself a book to read from his shelf. I picked out a long poem by Alfred Lord Tennyson. It was either *The Princess* or *The Idylls of the King.* I went for a walk down to Avondale Lake and read the book sitting on a bench under a brilliant orange maple tree, with the sky glowing on the water. I'd be lying if I said I remembered which passage impressed me, but it was probably one like this from *The Princess*:

> ∴ *Then rode we with the old king across the*
> *Lawns*
> *Beneath huge trees, a thousand rings of Spring*
> *In every bole, a song on every spray*
> *Of birds that piped their Valentines, and woke*
> *Desire in me to infuse my tale of love…*
> *And blossom-fragrant slipt the heavy dews*
> *Gather'd by night and peace, with each light*
> *Air*
> *On our mail'd head . . .****

After a few minutes, I looked up and began to tremble. I don't know if I fully understood what I was reading. It didn't matter to me then how the story went: I drank in the sound of the words, feeling them run down into my heart like fresh water. The water rose up and became a river rushing toward the most beautiful place in eternity: a garden under great, ancient trees where birds sang and "blossom-fragrant slipt the heavy dews." It was a vision of heavenly beauty, of timelessness and glory.

I swallowed tears and put my head back, staring up at this sky. It reminded me of the old joy of breaking a brick almost as if by magic—splintering the door of heaven for a second, getting a glimpse of something more real than what has always seemed real. Until this moment, it had been out of reach.

I wanted to tell someone how beautiful it was, but you can't pass an experience of beauty around like a good joke or a box of candy. You can't force people to adopt a love of yours, any more than you get them to enjoy your vacation pictures. Your only hope is to create a new experience for them from the old—like forms from the imagination of God reproducing themselves in types, which is one purpose of good conversation, and of art.

The promising thing, though, was that this vision of beauty had come to me directly. Yes, the words of the poem had provoked it, but still I had found that poem myself, and I had taken it to heart, and the feeling that stayed with me for several days was all mine—not inspired in me by parent, teacher, friend, or brother. I realized that I had an independent imagination. I could open my eyes and see something lovely without first being led to it by someone else.

A long time would pass before I had other visions of my own. I was too caught up in the people I loved to pursue my own joys, to find the places where their loves ended and mine began. But that day was miraculous: the glory of heaven pushed through slender cracks in the world, like a bird shaking away a shell. God gave me a brief glimpse of himself. In the words of another poem, I had a vision of paradise; in a moment of time, I saw the eternal.

> *The heavens declare the glory of God, and the firmament showeth his handiwork. Day unto day uttereth speech, and night unto night showeth knowledge. There is no speech nor language, where their voice is not heard.*****

9

walking
in shadows

Betty with friend, dressed as June Cleaver
for senior banquet, 1983

I am gall, I am heartburn. God's most deep decree
Bitter would have me taste: my taste was me . . .

—Gerard Manley Hopkins

Here was the irony of my teenage years: I lied constantly, and yet I loved the truth. In the same way that I wanted to look behind the curtain of time into the eternal and beautiful, I wanted to push aside lies and see what was real. I had my mother's urge to know things for what they were, even if the knowing was hard. And above all I wanted to be known.

But when I was fifteen and sixteen years old, that seemed impossible to arrange. I couldn't imagine living an open, honest life. I thought I had to choose between anonymity and deception.

At Avondale High School, I got my fill of anonymity. Half of the students were hauled in from elsewhere on packed buses. Big guards with guns walked the halls, regarding us with disinterest. We were cattle being herded through holding pens. I had no friends there, and only two of my teachers ever learned my first name.

After a year at Avondale, I begged my parents to let me leave and send me somewhere else, even if it was Covington Hills, the fundamentalist high school in the neighborhood where I'd have to wear culottes in gym class so as not to tempt somebody with my white knees. Mama at first fretted about the cost. "How would we afford private school with your sister in college?"

"Money's not the real problem," Daddy said. "I think she may need to stick this out for her own good." He brought up his World War II service against the Nazi Empire as an example. At that point I began crying and Mama weighed back in on my side, saying I'd inherited her sensitive nature and needed a gentler, less stressful environment. In the end they sent me off to LaVista Academy, a school run by the Missionary Alliance Church. It was also the preferred Christian school of conservative Atlanta Presbyterians.

LaVista was a startling change from Avondale High. Anonymity vanished, as did buses and guards and guns. I found myself in the bright glow of evangelical warmth. The teachers here not only knew our names, they knew where we went to church and what our fathers did for a living. They cared about our emotions; they cared even more about our souls. My algebra teacher would be writing a problem on the board; suddenly she would put down her chalk and wipe her eyes. "Y'all, I need to stop and share a little something with you from my heart. Put away your math books and get out your Bibles. . . ."

Changing over to a Christian school was like being hungry and stepping into a bakery. A candy shell of friendliness sweetened the whole surface of the place. Faculty and staff were cheerful and familial. The principal greeted us in the halls; he visited our classes and called us together for chapel on Wednesdays in the gym. Sometimes after long services we were allowed to scatter to the rooms of various teachers for "discipling." I felt my hopes rise at this school. Maybe I'd be happy here. Maybe this was how it felt to be *known*.

Just a couple of years after I graduated from high school, I came across a girl who'd been two classes ahead of me at LaVista: she'd been a super-spiritual type—leading Bible studies, playing choruses on her guitar in chapel, going on mission projects to Central America. Now she was a barmaid at the Mexicali Cactus. When she brought me a margarita, I asked her if she'd ever been back to the school to visit our old teachers.

"That school f—— me up so bad," she said, and flounced off. I sat in shock, wondering what had turned her from a smiling, perky evangelical to an angry cocktail waitress. It may have been something truly terrible; or it may have been simply a bitter intrusion of reality, a moment when she saw the contrast between the promise of Christian love and the facts of human weakness.

We'll love you unconditionally, evangelicals say to the convert or the new church member or the new student at a Christian school. They smile and extend the hands of fellowship, pulling the refugee or the exile into the Body of Christ: *You won't be lonely among us—we'll love you with the love of Jesus. We'll stick by you like family.* It's a fine hope they offer—the ideal of community, one of the great strengths of the evangelical church. To an extent the hope is realized. But human nature almost always adds its own conditions: *We'll love you as long as you're like us, as long as you don't disturb our comfort, don't threaten our beliefs, don't shame us.*

I knew that what passed for Christian love was often a mix of good intentions and good acting. I'd seen, for instance, the way our church people treated the preacher's wife, showing her kindness in public but criticizing her privately because she wasn't like them. Their kindness was all at the surface. When she tested it, it proved thin.

Because I wanted kindness, however thin it might be, I didn't test the surface of this new place. I took the warmth as it was offered to me, working hard to please the friendly teachers and the nice administrators. Whatever I did on my own time, at school I acted the part of an upright Christian teenager: president of the National Honor

Society, representative to the Governor's Honors Program, class valedictorian, etc.

At home, too, I tried to act like the daughter I knew my parents wanted. I read my Bible and sang in the choir and helped with the church's Vacation Bible School in Cabbage Town (a poor neighborhood). I went to Thursday youth group at our pastor's house and frequent parties with friends from LaVista Academy, but, unlike my popular sister before me, I had few dates, no boyfriends. I drove away the one boy from church who showed interested in me.

"I think I like you," he told me as we were eating chocolate mousse at a French restaurant. I looked up at him and felt my left eye twitch.

"I'm sorry, but I like someone else," I said, which was true. I liked an older boy who never learned my name and later turned out to be gay. My virtue, at least, was safe in high school. On Saturday nights you could usually find me in a chair, watching *The Love Boat*. As far as Mama knew, the main drama of my teenage years was ongoing loneliness.

And she was right. I went places, I did things, but I felt alone and unknown.

"What kind of girls *are* popular?" Mama would say, when she noticed I didn't get asked out much. "Is it like it was in my day, when the girls who dressed in the most fashionable clothes had all the boys interested in them?"

"Sort of."

"I'd like to get you some new outfits, Betty. Do you think that would help?"

I knew that she imagined me in soft, feminine dresses—Laura Ashley, maybe, or a similar off-brand: pastel blues and pinks and green. She thought of me as her nice Christian daughter who should be sipping sodas on Saturday nights with a fine Christian boy, perhaps the son of some Presbyterian executive. How could my mother, who'd been a teenager during World War II, be expected to understand high school life in the early 1980s—even among Christians? How could I tell her what went on at parties, the heavy drinking and occasional pot-smoking and ubiquitous coupling up? I suppose that the kids I hung out with were normal for their time (in pre-AIDS, pre-MADD America), but my Mama wasn't from their time, or anywhere near it. I knew she wouldn't be able to hold up—she might actually die—if certain truths about my life at high school were revealed.

And looking back, I realize that I felt as unknown in that high school partying life as I did with my parents and teachers. My wild friends accepted me well: they liked me because I was a ham and a daredevil, a B-52 wannabe (for a short time I was the lead singer of a punk band we put together, called the "VO5s"; I strummed an electric guitar and danced around in a tall wig and a floor-length navy dress from my church clothes closet). And they liked having an A student around: I tutored some of them in French and Latin and on at least one occasion wrote a friend's term paper. I was, predictably, the group's mascot and front woman, the preacher's daughter and honor student who legitimized things in the eyes of the adults around us.

But my friends didn't know me and I didn't know them, though I was their constant observer. At their parties I sat alone in a corner and watched them laugh, drink, dance (sometimes I danced, too—especially to "Rock Lobster"), pair off, slip away into dark places together. Meanwhile I drank what was offered and kept drinking it until I'd drifted into the comfort of complete anonymity. I craved this heavy, peaceful feeling of distance from the world—the gift of alcohol to those of us who usually try too hard to belong to it. As the nights wore on the others moved here and there like people in a film, talking to each other far away and with the volume turned low and fuzzy. It was easy to forget that they were even real. I stared and smiled and drank till I felt nothing.

One night at my friend Donny's house, after getting very drunk on peppermint schnapps, I went upstairs and locked myself in a dark bedroom alone. I heard shouting and laughing, but it seemed to have nothing to do with me. I crawled into the bed and slept. The next morning I threw up three times, then went downstairs and found them all sleeping around the living room—ten or eleven of them lying splayed out over chairs and across the carpet. I picked my way through the bodies and walked outside into the sunshine, squinting. My parents were both out of town on a church trip, so there was no danger in going home. I drove back to my empty house and got sick all over again. I was about to go back to bed, and then the doorbell rang.

I looked out the window. A couple stood on the front porch smiling, two wholesome-looking people in shorts and rugby shirts. They had suitcases with them. I opened the door and coughed into my hand.

I must have looked awful. The woman gave me a concerned smile. "Hi. Did your mom and dad tell you we were coming?"

"No, I don't think so." I tried to remember, but nothing came clear.

"We're missionaries," she said. "We're staying here over the weekend."

"Come in," I said. "It's fine." I moved aside to let them in. "I have the flu or something."

"I'm sorry," said the woman in a kind voice. She put a hand on my shoulder and smiled. I don't know if it was because of her gentleness or because she'd caught me at a weak moment: suddenly I had a great compulsion to open myself up to her. I pictured myself starting to speak and the words spurting from my mouth in loud, uncontrollable bursts "I have a hangover! It's my third one this month!" Was it possible that she'd hear me without freaking out? That she'd listen and I'd be glad afterwards because I'd told her the truth about myself? That I wouldn't feel ashamed and afraid?

"Do you need anything?" she asked me, looking right into my eyes.

"No, I don't think so," I said, and then I pulled my eyes away and went back to my room alone. For now, I chose to stay unknown.

High school ended with our senior production, *The Robe*, which has to be one of the worst plays of all time in any language. Our trigonometry teacher, Mrs. Flemigan, directed it, and nearly everyone in my class had a part. Luckily for us, it had been written for an era when bad acting was expected. I was the female lead, and my lines were all meant for a 1950s-style siren, a Lana Turner or a Susan Hayward.

"Marcellus," I was supposed to call dramatically from my bench at the side of the stage, "let's bribe a boat! Go someplace where no one's insane!" Then I was to run across the stage into Marcellus' arms and kiss him madly until the Emperor Caligula—my friend Donny—walked on stage and interrupted us.

I had a hard time battling my cynicism about all this: the lines made me laugh and my costumes made me look fat. But I wanted to throw myself into the part, anyway. I wanted to *be* the leading lady, really and truly in love with Marcellus, my leading man. He was a guy named Nate, a handsome missionary kid who'd grown up mainly in French West Africa, on the Ivory Coast. I knew him from parties and carpool and journalism class, though we'd never had a deep conversation. Our first kiss one day in rehearsal was the first kiss of my life. He thrust his lips down to mine and I jumped away in shock.

"I am so sure," said one of the Roman matrons behind me.

"Cut!" yelled Mrs. Flemigan. "That was *very* awkward. What's the matter with y'all?" Mrs. Flemigan walked to the front of the gym, her pointy high heels clipping on the wood floor, the lace of her Victorian blouse flapping.

"Can I talk to you privately?" I said.

We went out into the hall.

"It's the way he kissed me," I said. "I didn't expect—"

"I understand," she said. "Leave it to me." She marched back out front. "Marcellus, keep your tongue to yourself!"

Nate smirked. I felt my ears go red. I walked up to the stage again, holding my head down. I sat on the bench and tried to get into character. It was almost time for my line again. Here it came . . .

"Marcellus, let's bribe a boat! Go someplace where no one's insane!"

Step, step, step, kiss. I cringed in horror. I knew he felt me tensing up. I pulled back when he tried to reach my lips. He groaned.

"I'm sorry," I said. "I'm so sorry."

Over the next few days we practiced the kiss repeatedly. Each time, as soon as Donny strode onto stage in the Caligula armor, I kissed Nate quickly and then broke from him like a layer of mud crumbling off of a statue. He was furious. Outside of rehearsals, he wouldn't talk to me at all.

On the evening of the performance, I walked out into the woods by the school pond in my silly purple toga and picked myself some wisteria blossoms to put in my hair. Wisteria's not usually an ideal headpiece for stage drama. From a distance it looks like a cluster of grapes draped over your head, and the smell can make you sneeze. Just the name "wisteria," though, sounded promising to me at that moment: it brought to mind other words: "wistful," "wishful," "whimsical." It sounded romantic, and I needed to be my most romantic, least cynical self tonight. The afternoon was especially beautiful. The sky over the trees was streaked with blue and pink like a huge hydrangea bush. The lawns around the school were still cottony with dogwoods. I went back in to the rehearsal room, where the cast was getting ready.

"Tonight," said Mrs. Flemigan, "we are not just doing any old play. Y'all, we are doing a play that may actually lead people out in that audience to the Lord. Just think about the meaning y'all are trying to get across. This is the gospel. Think about how at first Marcellus doesn't believe in Jesus. He doesn't believe the robe of Jesus is anything special. But then God shows him that this Jesus is real, and that he's the Savior. We just need to pray for the people out in the audience. 'Cause y'all, God can change their hearts, too. I want you to think about that. Y'all are a missionary team."

I looked around. Over there in the corner stood Nate in his cape and red-plumed helmet; Donny as Caligula in his plastic breastplate; my punk friend Mike with his hair spiked up; another friend Eric, who'd deflowered several of the girls in the room; and all the others, all the rest of my class gathered in this one place and dressed in bedsheet togas. A handful of kids—quiet girls, mainly—might have qualified as young missionaries; most of us were a show within a show, acting out other people's ideal of Christian youth.

But the greater (or maybe lesser) show went on. My mother and brother Danny were out in the audience that night, and I was nervous. I knew what my brother would be thinking about this crappy play. Somehow thinking of him—knowing how Danny would laugh at that awful line ("someplace where no one's insane!") freed me a little from nervousness. When I ran into Nate's arms, I kissed him as hard as I could. Two or three seconds into the kiss, we heard "oomphs" and huffing sounds backstage. Caligula couldn't get his armor on.

"Hey!" I heard Donny stage whisper to somebody. "Help me! Over here!"

It was a very long kiss, but not long enough to get Caligula on stage. Finally, I pulled myself away from Nate and stood looking at him from under my wisteria blossoms, smiling and trying not to laugh. He smiled back at me. It felt good to have this private joke: a moment of real connection between us, when, in spite of the face paint and the ridiculous costumes, we became real. In the middle of an elaborate farce, we had one honest moment. For the remainder of the play I thought about Nate and wondered if anything would come of that kiss.

Nothing did, of course. When the show was over and the gym cleaned up, the chairs put away and the cast party finished, Nate left with the girl who'd been our stage manager. I spent the rest of the night in a less elaborate farce—in the corner of someone's living room, floating on alcohol and unhappiness. I was well on my way to a career as a cocktail waitress.

Yet with some God-given spark of faith, I kept hoping, in spite of everything, that it was possible to be known, and that someone would be concerned enough to discover the truth about me. I felt like a mummy in a cave. I longed to be honest and free—longed for someone to hunt me down, find me, break through to this dark little space I was lying in, and pull me up to the light.

"I want *You*," I was saying, without any idea who might respond.

10
the path
of restlessness

Great art thou, O Lord, and greatly to be praised;
great is thy power, and thy wisdom is infinite. And man
wants to praise you, man who is only a small portion of
what you have created and who goes about carrying with
him his own mortality, the evidence of his own sin and
evidence that Thou resistest the proud. Yet still man, this
small portion of creation, wants to praise you. You stimu-
late him to take pleasure in praising you, because you have
made us for yourself, and our hearts are restless until they
can find peace in you.

—St. Augustine, *Confessions*

In the fall of 1983, I took my cynical self north to
Wheaton College, the very flower of evangelical Christianity.
The school had a fine academic reputation, but it was best
known for turning out missionaries, evangelists, and martyrs,
not to mention the odd Republican politician. Four times a
week the Edman Chapel chimes called the student body
together to be addressed by evangelicalism's finest: Billy

Graham, Francis Schaeffer, Charles Colson—all the great heroes of our branch of Christendom drifting over the chapel stage like floats in a slow-motion parade. Wheaton wasn't Presbyterian or even Reformed, but it differed little from the culture I already knew so well. It allowed no drinking or smoking or dancing (except chaste square-dancing such as had been practiced across the northern Illinois prairie for nigh on one hundred and fifty years); it encouraged Christian dating and marriage but prohibited all forms of hanky-panky. The unofficial motto of the school was "in loco parentis," which meant that I wasn't supposed to do anything there to bring shame upon my Mama and Daddy, and if I did, I'd be sent home on the next bus out of Chicago.

My love for Wheaton is now so great that it's hard to remember why I disliked it when I first went. But I did. What caused me to choose such a vibrantly Christian college in the first place, I cannot tell, except that my brother Danny had gone there in the early 1970s and had come back making it sound like heaven on earth. Maybe I thought I'd follow a similar path. I'd leave home a lonely and confused teenager and come back a happy, well-rounded adult. As for my Christianity, I'd continue on the path I'd ⌐ ırted down in high school, playing the part of small-time rebel and cynic, only without having to deceive anyone about it. My family would be hundreds of miles away. I could let my new friends see me as I was. Emotionally speaking, I'd no longer feel alone.

To earn money for my freshman year, I spent my last summer at home working at my father's mission office. I sat all day at a computer terminal, inputting donor addresses and contributions to the missionaries. Occasionally I'd figure out that I'd had my fingers on the wrong keys for the last hour or so and typed things like "Vimmomhjs" instead of "Cunningham." The job obviously didn't occupy a lot of my imagination. I spent most of my creative energies on social relationships within the office: trading stories and jokes, taking sinfully long lunches and breaks. I liked all the people there, and I soon began to devote myself to a particular friendship with an older co-worker, an interesting person who had a sad history, a mysterious life to be explored, imagined, and uncovered. I'd been down this road several times now, most memorably with the karate teacher and the preacher's wife, but also with schoolteachers and various other older friends. I was beginning to understand that the road always looked the same.

First I met someone who seemed competent and happy; after a short time, though, I sensed that he or she (usually she) had some hidden pain in the past: a buried tragedy that still caused her great suffering. I next set about discovering what the tragedy was. Once I'd discovered it, I responded with huge sympathy, so fully that I thought about almost nothing else. I suffered vicariously over each of her hurts. If she allowed me to, I did everything I could to make up for them, acting like an overprotective mother, or a devoted child.

The tragedy of this new friend's life was that she'd loved a succession of bad men who'd used her in various ways but didn't love her. She was now over thirty and wondering if she'd be alone forever. Though she worked very hard, she barely made enough money to support herself, and much of that she gave away to her church.

So maybe I could help her out: find her a husband! Make her rich! After some consideration, I realized I couldn't do either. One night, though, I drove to her house in secret and left some money under a wiper blade of her car: one hundred dollars of my hard-earned college savings. By the next day the news about the money had gotten around the office. Apparently, this gift had scared my friend. She was afraid it came from a strange guy who was obsessed with her. Everyone else in the office was busy sympathizing with her fears, wondering aloud: What kind of weirdo would leave that much money on a car with a note that said, "Spend this however you want"? I hadn't expected this reaction.

"It could be a neighbor," said somebody. "We had a neighbor who looked in our trash at night."

"Ooh! That is weird," said somebody else.

"He could be dangerous. I'd definitely give the note and the money to the police."

This was an odd experience, hearing myself discussed so objectively. I felt as if I were coming to consciousness in the middle of an operation, listening to the doctors exclaim over my internal organs: "Good Lord! Have you ever seen one like this?" Apparently I was a freak of nature; everything they said about the hypothetical weirdo, I applied to myself. I was indeed dangerous; I was obsessed. While everyone else managed to keep their loves in check, I couldn't stop myself from loving some people too much.

No one ever found out that I'd given that money, and the lesson I took away from the event was *Try not to love people too obviously. Do not let this side of yourself be known.*

At the end of the summer, I said good-bye to people at the office, trying to pretend I was excited about going to college, not all that bothered about leaving my old life behind. But when I hugged my best friend (recipient of the secret gift) I felt a strong surge of homesickness. It was the old ache of exile, of impending separation. Mama and Daddy drove me from Atlanta to Wheaton themselves, with Daddy's World War II footlocker packed for a polar expedition: Mama had bought me a very large coat, a heavy scarf, gloves, knit cap, thermal underwear, numerous sweaters, and even wool socks. She had knitted me a pair of slippers that looked like large booties. On the way we spent one night in a double room at a motel somewhere off the Interstate near the

Indiana/Illinois line. The next day we drove to Wheaton and pulled up at the college just as freshman orientation was getting started on the quad. Big signs announced, "Freshman chapel tonight! Hymn sing! Prayer with R.A.'s!"

My mother put her arm around my waist. "It's going to be hard to leave you, Betty."

From a dorm window above us, Amy Grant sang, *Her father's eyes, her father's eyes, her father's eyes, she's got her father's eyes. . . .** I felt myself slipping into something like shock. Why had I decided to leave behind my home, my family, and above all my beloved friend in order to come to this place that seemed like nothing so much as a great big youth group meeting, a church service that would go on for four years? And now my parents were smiling and leading me to my dorm room, unpacking, putting away clothes. My father was puttering around, introducing himself to people.

I thought, "I've died and gone to Christianity hell."

The next morning, Daddy was in a hurry to get home. He and Mama came to say good-bye behind my dorm. Daddy kissed me. Mama hugged me. We waved at each other and then suddenly I lost my composure and burst into tears. Mama came back and threw her arms around me. I sobbed on her shoulder.

"I don't want to stay here!" I said. "I want to go home!"

She looked mystified. "Why? What's wrong?"

"I don't know." I meant, as usual, that I didn't have the

courage to explain. I felt like a little girl again, crying for my mother at night.

"Please don't cry like this," Mama said. "We can't stand to leave you so miserable."

"Mama, I wish I could come *home* with you. "

She stood back and looked at me, close to tears, herself. "You can come home anytime," she said. "Right, Ken?"

"Right," said my father a few feet away, raising his eyebrows. But he sounded sincere.

My mother patted me some more. Then she and my father got into their car and drove off toward home. I sat down on a curb and cried. What would have happened if I'd chased their car as it crept away down the street, if I'd begged them to take me back to Atlanta? I wanted to, but something stopped me: a sense of a door closing on the past, a definite ending. My fate could no longer be so closely bound up with the fates of the people who had brought me into the world. I felt this strongly, and it only added to the homesickness. I could never go back, not really.

I went to my room and called my friend back home and talked to her for forty-five minutes at daytime rates. After that expensive call, I visited the college counselor. He handed me tissue after tissue, listening to me and occasionally saying, "That's not neat." Then he gave me a prescription for Valium so that I could calm down. I went back to the dorm and fell into a zombie-like trance for about a week. I was the walking unconscious. When I came out of it, they told me I'd passed through freshman orientation with flying colors: I'd square-danced, scavenger-hunted, played flag football. I was ready to begin what Wheaton people called "The Integration of Faith and Learning."

There's really only one way to enjoy a Christian college, and that's actually to be a Christian. On one of my first days there, we had a prayer meeting on our floor. Out of about twenty girls, I was the only one who didn't pray aloud. I sat on my blue upholstered chair in the dorm lobby, squinting at the other girls in the prayer circle. They all sat as still as statues of saints, backs straight, eyelids closed, heads bowed in piety. That same night, our Resident Advisor asked all the girls to come to her room for a Bible study and foot-washing. I thought it sounded like the most embarrassing thing imaginable: worse than doing a striptease in the middle of church. So I skipped. The next day, the dorm director came to my room and sat beside me on my bed. "I hear you're a little homesick."

"I guess so," I said.

"Do you like Wheaton?"

"It feels like Christian camp," I said. "It's not what I expected."

She narrowed her eyebrows. "It's OK to be homesick. That's very normal. But by Christmas, I promise you'll be telling me, 'Wheaton is my real home now.'"

I didn't know what to say to say to that. I thought there wasn't a chance in the world. There wasn't a chance in the universe.

"I was homesick like you once," she said, "and look at me now." She pointed at an engagement ring on her finger.

I shook my head and started crying again. "I've screwed up, I've wasted my parents' money, and I'm going to disappoint them."

"No, you aren't! You're going to do great. Do you hear me?" She prayed aloud and then gave me a long hug and left. I sat looking out the window at the parking lot by the dorm, wondering if there were any other people at this college who weren't fanatically odd—who didn't want to go to prayer meetings, or get their feet washed, or stop longing for friends and family and think of Wheaton as their real home now. By this time I'd already spent huge amounts, probably hundreds of dollars of my parents' money, on long-distance phone calls. Wasn't there anyone else here who felt as out of place as I did?

My roommate and I didn't have enough in common for a friendship to form between us. She'd decorated her side of the room with religious posters: pictures of puppies and rainbows and forest scenes framed by quotations from the Bible: "This is the Day the Lord has Made. We will Rejoice and Be Glad in It." She'd told me she was here at Wheaton to find a Christian husband. No, she never listened to rock-and-roll music, only the Carpenters and a little bit of Debby Boone and gospel quartets—oh, and the children's story hour on the Moody Bible radio station. I told her that I didn't care for any of that, but that I didn't mind what she listened to, because I had headphones.

Over the next weeks, she and I sat studying in our little room on the first floor of Evans Dorm, she listening to Karen Carpenter and I hiding in my headphones, which were old and as big as coconuts. I read *The Brothers Karamazov* over the Brahms *Requiem*; I translated Horace while listening to the English Beat. Sometimes I ventured out of the room and tried to meet new people. I met a girl named Pam who'd grown up in Japan, the daughter of missionaries. She was as homesick as I was. "In Japan . . . ," she would say, and I would reply antiphonally with, "Well, in the South. . . ." Gradually, I met a few other girls, most of them unhappy, too. We all got together, threw our grief into a pot, and stirred it up. Unfortunately, though misery may love company, it would always prefer a bottle of cheap wine and a pack of Lucky Strikes. Naturally, the college snack bar didn't offer either of those.

Meanwhile, the days grew shorter and darker. The wind became frigid and made the tears freeze in our eyes as we walked from classroom to dining hall to dorm. In October we had our first big snowstorm. I waddled between classes in my enormous coat and rubber boots. I tramped downtown through the snow and had hot coffee at the Round the Clock diner. The weather was both miserable and exhilarating. I reconciled myself to it. Before long I'd exchanged the big coat for a heavy sweater and blue-jean jacket.

But still I could not reconcile myself to the most central element of the place: the inescapable, unassailable, evangelical Christianity. I felt it everywhere: everyone talked it, everyone lived by it, and nearly everyone believed it. It wasn't theology: it was an atmosphere fed by the school's missionary zeal and blown into turbulence by the uniform behavior and thought of thousands of people. It would lie heavy and still for a while—almost forgotten in the rush of term papers and exams—and then suddenly it would sweep up and blow over the college like a blizzard, blanketing classrooms, hissing in the dorm radiators, wailing through the windows of the dining hall. Not only were we to act like Christians Triumphant (avoid sin, pray without ceasing, do good works), but we were to think like Christians Triumphant (believe all the Scriptures, embrace orthodoxy, love God above everything, desire holiness rather than worldly pleasures). The time of decision about faith was assumed to be in the past. Our place now was not to wrestle and struggle, but to prepare ourselves to carry the cross of Christ into the greater world. We'd all grown up singing, *Onward Christian soldiers. . . . Soldiers of Christ arise and put your armor on. . . . We are marching to Zion. . . .* We'd been taught to imagine an invisible army arrayed against us, with Satan at its head. Our time at Wheaton was to be military training: the cross here was a symbol of overcoming rather than suffering.

So why hadn't anybody who knew me well—my brother Danny, for instance—warned me that Wheaton would be like this? I don't think anyone realized the extent to which I'd left my faith behind. I'd had my mother and friends around to keep me rooted in the world I'd grown up with—to give me the sameness and stability that I might have looked for, otherwise, in God. I could have lived that way for a long time, being outwardly faithful though inwardly cynical. But when I'd said good-bye to my parents, my exile from God was complete. There was no longer anything cozy or familiar about Christianity.

The religion at Wheaton felt like a brittle wind blowing across my neck. I reacted to it in one sense by marching defiantly forward, refusing to conform. I kept beer in my room, smoked cigarettes, went to clubs in Chicago with friends I'd met at my part-time job. But if I'd wanted the freedom to drink and smoke, I could have gone to a thousand other colleges. I wished I had the courage to do something outward and honest and definitely wrong. It would be a self-defining sin, a declaration of independence against the entire evangelical world. *I will not*, I would say (if only in deed), *live my life as an unquestioning, hypocritical pawn like the rest of you.*

For a while I fantasized about having a torrid affair with a professor. I suppose I knew it would remain a fantasy, but entertaining sexual thoughts seemed outrageous here, where virginity was practically an admission requirement. I looked around for somebody attractive to proposition, at the same time taking stock of my appearance: I'd had my hair permed recently and looked like Richard Simmons.

My favorite professor at the moment was the man who reminded me of John F. Kennedy. He taught a required freshman course called "Theology of Culture." Never had I been so impressed by a teacher's knowledge—actually, his authority in the classroom. He had a forceful, dramatic teaching style. He clearly believed what he said, which made him all the more attractive as an object of decadence. I wanted his attention. The problem was that so far I had a boring B+ in his class.

I made a private appointment to see him in his office: I imagined flirting with him in a quiet spot, luring him away from his books.

"What did you want to talk about?" he asked me, when I actually sat down with him a few days later.

I felt my lips tremble. I'd seen myself saying something like, "You have beautiful blue eyes." But he was giving me such a steely stare. He looked uncomfortable with the closeness: I thought he probably preferred the distance of the class-room. I gazed around the room at his books and settled my eyes on the shiny top of his round table. "Well, it's hard to explain. . . ."

"Are you enjoying the class?" he said.

"I'm having a hard time believing some things."

"What things?"

"Such as, that God even really exists."

"Oh, I see." He nodded knowingly. "Is that why you came to talk to me?"

It hadn't been, but now it was. I nodded.

"Well, there are several ways to approach this. But here's what I want you to do. First of all, I want you to think about your relationship with your father. "

"With my father? Is that important?"

"That's right. Think about that. And then I want you to come back in a few days and tell me what you think."

I squinted at him. "Tell you what I think about my father?"

"Yes. You may not understand it right now. But how you think about your father, that's how you think about God."

"Really?"

"Yes. Your father represents God. So think about that. I'll see you in a few days."

I left his office without offering myself. I went to the snack bar, bought some coffee, and sat for a moment thinking about my relationship with my father. Nothing profound came to my mind. I liked my father. He liked me. What more could you ask? Three days later, in class, my professor assigned us readings from works by famous theologians.

"How many of you have ever heard of Tertullian?" he asked us. "How about Anselm or Abelard? Søren Kierkegaard? Wow. Nobody's heard of Søren Kierkegaard. Well, how about Karl Barth? How about Paul Tillich? Raise your hands if you know these names. Most of you from Christian families and none of you know these names. Shocking. Distressing."

I wanted so much to raise my hand, but I was afraid he'd call on me and ask something like, "So what was Tertullian's first name?"

"How about Martin Luther?" he said. "John Calvin?"

I launched my hand into the air.

"Obviously," he said with a patronizing smile. "As I expected."

I retracted my hand a little.

"Well," he said. "Go back and read Augustine's *Confessions* over the weekend. We'll talk about it on Monday."

I went to him as everyone drained from the room and made arrangements to speak with him later in the day in his office. It was dusk outside when I sat down across from him in Blanchard Hall. The air in his office felt heavy. I could see people walking back and forth on the other side of his clouded glass door.

"So," he said, "what did we say we were going to talk about?"

I was disappointed that he didn't remember. "You wanted me to tell you how I get along with my father."

"That's right. Go ahead."

"Well, I've thought about it. . . ." I began to talk, and I talked more than he'd probably wanted me to. I explained that I loved my dad, and that he was a great preacher. I said that he did travel a lot, so we'd never spent loads of time together. I told him that my mother and I were very close and that I missed her. I told him about my high school unhappiness and my obsessive friendships, the way I clung so hard to some people while I kept a distance from others. I told him that right now I was very homesick for a friend of mine back in Atlanta. And I told him that I felt ugly and awkward and that I seemed to be way out of place at the college. "I hate myself," I said. "And I hate this place. I really do. It seems so fake."

He nodded. "To you, God is very, very far away. You can't love someone who won't come close."

"I can't even believe in God, much less love him."

"I want you to think now about the fatherhood of God. Meditate on that. A father is very important because he tells you who you really are—as a person, as a woman. I want you to think about God as a father and then come back and tell me what you've discovered."

"Is that all?"

"I'd like to give you some Scripture and some books."

"OK."

"Your assignment is prayer, and meditation, and some reading."

I was disappointed. I didn't want to meditate or read the Bible. I wanted to talk some more. I wanted a relationship with him. I wanted his attention.

"Think and pray," he said. "And I'll see you in class."

That weekend, I didn't read the Bible. I'd decided to be through with Bible reading for a while. Instead I read our assigned text, *The Confessions of St. Augustine*. I knew nothing about the African saint, except that they'd named a city in Florida for him. I was a minister's daughter with years and years of Christian education behind me, and yet the sad fact was that in our education we'd pretty much skipped from St. Paul to the Reformation. So I opened up the *Confessions* for the first time and read that famous beginning passage:

> *Yet still man, this small portion of creation, wants to praise you. You stimulate him to take pleasure in praising you, because you have made us for yourself, and our hearts are restless until they can find peace in you.* **

From a religious point of view, those words weren't applicable to me. I didn't want to praise God, I wanted to ignore him. I understood, though, what it meant to be restless at heart. I understood the desire for peace. Even now I felt restless and tired: I wanted to live by truth rather than lies. I wanted to trust that if I stopped piling up layers of deceit—stopped hiding myself from people around me, who might consider me sinful, or sick, or both—then the deluge of misery wouldn't break through. Yet here I'd gone and landed myself in the unambiguous capital of victorious Christianity where more than ever I felt the need to hide. How could this place survive intact if it admitted restlessness? Restlessness was essentially unfulfilled desire, and the evangelical approach to desire was always control: control founded in belief and faith. If you had desire without belief and faith, you could get yourself in powerful trouble. You could bring the world down around you.

> I came to Carthage [said Augustine, a few chapters later], and all around me in my ears were the sizzling and frying of unholy loves, I was not yet in love, but I loved the idea of love, and from a hidden want I hated myself for not wanting more. Being in love with love I looked for something to love; I hated security and a path without snares. I was starved inside me for inner food (for yourself, my God). . . . And for this reason my soul was in poor health;

it burst out into feverish spots which brought the wretched longing to be scratched by contact with the objects of sense. . . . It was a sweet thing to me both to love and to be loved. ***

Here I saw something important. Augustine realized that desire itself must betray our need for God.**** When he called God the "inner food" he'd been starved for as a young man, he implied that desire itself is God-given and holy— not a force to be smothered or controlled, but an instinct to be followed to its natural satisfaction. Desire is our map and restlessness is our compass. Their accurate destination is heaven.

At first, Augustine's words seemed more significant to me as an individual than as a member of a community. Had I not desired one person after another? Had I not felt starved for love and tried to ease that starvation with friendship? My hunger for people was certainly passionate and feverish. It brought me a feeling of "wretched longing" for the objects of my affection.

Then one day after reading the *Confessions*, I sat in chapel and had a sort of epiphany. I looked out to my left and right, in front of me and behind me, over those thousands of serious young faces, and I realized that behind so many of the faces must be minds and hearts, like mine, in turmoil. I'd thought of Wheaton evangelicals as hypocrites because they seemed so falsely positive. But they were being deceitful only in their behavior—not in their hopes, which were real. They honestly did want to be passionate about God. They wanted to be the strong, faithful people that they appeared to be when they prayed aloud at dorm meetings, when they sang, "The joy of the Lord is my strength!" and "What a mighty God we serve!" But hope and wanting are only paths: they don't bring those who hope immediately to their destinations. Restlessness is powerful and immediate, while God's Rest itself is long in coming. I felt that many of these people must be struggling, as Augustine had, to wait.

Instead of resenting them, I felt compassion for them. It was as if a great backdrop had fallen away at the front of the chapel and I saw the inner workings of the place: people worshiping, doubting, praying, turning in all directions, longing for God but unable to wait for God. The drama of the religious life was ancient, and evangelical culture with all its cheeriness and pageantry was another stage set. I left chapel feeling a burden lifted off of me: I didn't have to agree with these people, or accept all of their thinking, in order to sympathize. I could laugh at them for their excesses and love them for their hopes. I even smiled at the girl who tried to sign me up for the Young Republicans.

"No, thanks," I said, "I'm a registered Communist."

I met my theology professor those two times, and then, for some reason—probably because of a scheduling mistake—he missed our third meeting. I felt hurt, and I didn't try to schedule another. I didn't stop thinking about him, though, and about our conversations. In those short meetings and in his lectures to the class, he'd given me the very thing he sensed I didn't have—a longing for the love of God as a father. Like my own father, this man was a marvelous teacher, brave enough to carry the torch of knowledge before the benighted multitudes (in this case, people who'd never heard of Tertullian). He obviously felt less comfortable speaking with me face-to-face, and yet he did speak and listen, with great kindness. He treated me respectfully as a person with both a mind to be taught and a heart to be shepherded— treatment I'd never received from any man.

I felt more restless than ever, with new desires stirring up in me, gathering force like a far-off storm. At the same time, I had new joys that brought a measure of calm: good books to read, good teachers, a handful of promising friends. When I went back to Georgia after that first fiercely cold winter in Wheaton, the South had never seemed so lush and rolling and green. Every tall tree, every hill was a miracle. I walked down to Avondale Lake, the park where I had had a vision years before while reading Tennyson, but now instead of reading poetry I stared at the red clay banks and the dogwoods mirrored in the water. I'd learned that some good things will endure. Occasionally, by the grace of God, you can come back to the very place you think you've lost forever. . . .

11

Betty with Jon at Betty's graduation from Wheaton, 1987

incarnation

For most of us, there is only the unattended
Moment, the moment in and out of time,
The distraction fit, lost in a shaft of sunlight,
The wild thyme unseen, or the winter lightning
Or the waterfall, or music heard so deeply
That it is not heard at all, but you are the music
While the music lasts . . .
The hint half guessed, the gift half understood,
is Incarnation.

—T.S. Eliot, "Burnt Norton"

For Christians, the Incarnation is no ordinary doctrine: it lies at the center of everything. When God became man in Jesus, eternity married itself to time, heaven to earth, glory to imperfection. There's no flawless metaphor for this: we speak of the oak tree curled up in a tiny seed, we think of an enormous star collapsing into a small point of matter. The greatest things we can imagine, though, have physical boundaries. God has no boundaries, and that fact itself confounds sense; never mind trying to figure out how he could live in a body; how he could ask not to do his own will the night before his death (*let this cup pass from me*) and turn his back on himself when he died. We think of the mystery of the light—that it can be both a wave and a particle of energy at the same time. This contradiction reminds us of the Incarnation, but fails as a metaphor because it's so impersonal: it doesn't convey the love or the sacrifice of God, which the Incarnation is meant to do. I've always liked best the idea of an author writing himself into his own story, because I can imagine an author who loves his characters enough to enter their world. Then I remember Jesus on the cross: God literally dying. A human writer suffers nothing but a little anxiety for the people he creates. If they turn their backs on him, he can always toss his book aside and go to the movies.

We talked a lot about the Incarnation at Wheaton. Our teachers taught us to look everywhere for the general principle of "word made flesh," or universals made concrete. The physical world and even art itself contain manifestations of truth—what John Bunyan in his preface to *Pilgrim's Progress* called "Truth in swaddling [clothes]." As God dressed himself in a human body, truth dresses itself in parables and pictures. We find it in stories and the words of songs. We feel our lives swell to bursting with it: in our loves, in our passions, we are little pictures of eternity. Truth strains at the seams of this world. Nature is the incarnation of God's thoughts.

I absorbed this message from my teachers, but naturally I doubted it. Like so many doctrines, the Incarnation of Jesus seemed to me a beautiful idea, but perhaps no more than that. As for the broader Christian teaching of incarnation— that God has concealed or "incarnated" truths about himself in nature—I thought that this, too, was a great idea, but I didn't have any faith in it. It seemed to me just as likely that nature existed first, and that Christianity (in fact, all religions) created teachings about God from what could be observed in the world.

These are things I still wonder about in moments of religious angst, but in my early twenties the questions seemed overwhelming and profoundly upsetting. I was no longer so rebellious. I felt at peace with the world, and even with evangelicals. I wanted to believe in God, and anyway I'd never really stopped loving the idea of Jesus: that is, Jesus the real, particular man as pictured in the Bible, the one who'd said, "Come unto me, all ye that labor and are heavy laden, and I will give you rest."* Even when I doubted God's existence, I admired Christ and wanted so much to believe in his divinity. As a confirmed cynic, though, I argued with my own wanting. Thinking about the Incarnation was like getting a letter from a sweepstakes company: "Congratulations on being one of ten finalists for our ten-million-dollar prize!" Sounded great, but what were the chances? To admire a lovely idea is one thing; to embrace it may be wishful thinking.

I applied the same reasoning, meanwhile, to love. I admired the idea of love—yearned for it, actually. I wanted arms around me, deep sighs, passionate kisses. On warm nights, sometimes, lying in bed and unable to sleep, I put my arms out, crying, wanting so badly to have somebody to hold onto. It wasn't one person that I wanted, though that would be a good start. I felt as if I wanted to bring the whole world into myself: all of humanity, all of nature. I wanted to open up and reel in the sky, the silver clouds, the gray grass under the window. The world seemed to me a mass of individual and unrelated identities, everything separate and alone. If the past was unconnected to the present, which was unconnected to the future, then love and loyalty had no permanence: they were constantly changing, constantly shifting. Friendship and even family had no real lasting importance.

So I wanted to heal this fragmentation, first by opening up to love. I desired connection above everything else. The desire, though, seemed laughable. I wasn't even all that approachable, must less open and yielding. Who would ever come close enough to connect with me? Me—the girl with the sharp tongue, all brain and no Botticelli. It's not that I was hideous to look at; I could "clean up good," as we say in the South. And I wasn't cold certainly: I was passionate and loyal in friendship; I devoted myself sacrificially, often slavishly, to one female friend after another, getting my heart broken over a succession of petty hurts. But where men were concerned,

I had a hard, unscratchable surface. Except for the theology professor who had made such an impression on me, I didn't even find most men interesting. Already I'd scared off the one or two who pursued me. I yawned during conversations, fled away in the dining hall, rolled my eyes at their jokes, ridiculed them to my friends.

But I did desire men physically, and the beauty of physical desire is that you can't really contain it. It's instinct, I suppose. The urge is meant to bear fruit, and the first fruit it bears is hope. The gates of cynicism shall not prevail against it. I ridiculed men, but I couldn't help hoping for one to come close. So I hoped, and I hated myself for hoping, and afterward I hoped some more.

And then, it seems now as if by a miracle, the incarnation of hope sprang up before me. I call him that because I know what he became to me, but at the time he seemed like another potential disappointment. His name was Jon. He was twenty-two years old and slender as a reed. For some reason he seemed attracted to me: not to my test scores or my grades in Greek, though it didn't bother him, either, if I was good at some things. We got acquainted in a writing class. I admired his talent: I thought he was funny. We had coffee a few times and then one night he asked me to go for a walk. It was a cold February evening and snow was falling. White mist curled through the suburban streets, circling the necks of the trees like scarves. He told me that he'd been thinking about me for a long time, and that he wanted to know what I was thinking, because he was about to graduate and he had to make plans.

It was a romantic setting. We were all alone, tramping across a white baseball field through a veil of falling snow. I'd imagined myself in scenes like this, but I was too nervous to enjoy it. I felt my old fears coming on.

"What kind of plans are you trying to make?" I asked him.

"I need," he said slowly, "to know whether I should stay in the U.S. or go back to Japan." (Like my friend Pam—like half the people I knew at Wheaton—he'd grown up on the mission field. He was considering whether to return to the other side of the world.)

"I can't tell you what to do," I said. "That's a decision you have to make for yourself."

"But do you *want* me to stay?" He smiled significantly.

"Do *I* want you to? What do you mean?" I said, though I knew exactly what he meant, and it terrified me. Why would he do this to me, make me responsible for this? If I told him to stay, it might change the course of his life: screw it up, even. If I told him to go, I'd feel like an idiot—here was my chance maybe to find somebody to love. After so much self-pity and yearning, it would be foolish not to try. But I thought there was probably no chance. I wanted to tell him: *Don't expect much from me, because I'm not a normal girl.*

"If you want to stay in America," I said, "then you should stay. But you shouldn't do it for me."

"But what do you want? Do you think—?"

"Hey," I said, "are you asking me to be your girlfriend or something?"

He laughed. "Yes!"

My heart began to beat. Why had I said that? I wanted to go back home this minute.

"So would you be my girlfriend?" he said.

I stopped walking. Then he stopped, too. I nodded at the ground and gathered my courage. "Well," I said thoughtfully, as if he'd just made me a job offer, "I guess my answer is yes."

"That's great!" he said.

"I can't promise it'll work out, but I like you and I want to try."

"That's all I want you to do."

"OK," I said. So there it was, our possible future together, discussed and considered according to the rules of matter-of-factness, rather than passion.

I thought I noticed a bounce in his step as we reached campus. His hopes were apparently high. Fine, I thought, but what was I really supposed to "try" to do? What would he require of me? Was I going to try to love him? Should I hope he'd be happy with what I could give, even if it wasn't much? He came from a country where they had arranged marriages, after all. Maybe he'd be content with a girlfriend who only liked him casually.

We went back to my dorm and said good-bye. I went inside and up to the fourth floor. I looked out the window of my bedroom at the snow and the sky, still unable to believe it, to trust it. The whole thing made me so uneasy. It seemed to me like a strange dream.

Over the next few days, whenever I saw him I noticed how happy and awkward he looked. He tried to open doors the wrong way, he tripped over speed bumps. What was wrong with him? Did he have a nervous disorder? It seemed inconceivable that I could be the cause of such behavior, yet I worried that I was. Didn't people in love often act like that? I felt I needed to tone him down. Otherwise, how could I make this work? The warmer and more friendly he acted, the cooler and more distant I became.

We went out nearly every evening, sometimes taking long walks after we'd finished our studies. I noticed that his hair was too far down on his forehead and that his nose looked slightly larger on the right side than on the left; the holes of his ears weren't exactly what I thought they should be and his neck seemed a bit long. On the other hand, if I stood exactly in front of him and looked at him from perfectly straight on, I thought he was handsome. So I tried to stand exactly in front of him as often as possible. This could be my last chance at love. I would give it my best shot.

And truthfully, though I'd identified every last one of his imperfections, I knew that the problem was in me, not him.

Yes, I liked him so much, and yet I felt that all those years of burial and deception—the mountains of self-protection that had piled up since I was a little girl—held back that liking. My heart was dammed up. Part of it wanted to break open to him, but the other part wanted to hold back, contained. Part of me wanted to open up and draw him in, but the other part wanted to remain closed, hard, dead.

"If he would kiss me," I thought, "kiss me one time, maybe I would stop thinking constantly about his faults. I could get close to him and attached to him; I could love him."

I suppose I hoped that sexual or romantic longing would be on my side. If he kissed me, lightning would flash in my soul: love would rise up and walk on its own. But a month passed, then a month and a half, and he still hadn't kissed me. We wandered around deserted school buildings after dark; we looked out the fourth-floor windows of Blanchard Hall, over the snow. I kept standing close to him, exactly in front of him. Each time we met I stood closer. But Jon wouldn't kiss me. He held my hand and told me he loved me, but he didn't kiss me.

One night we stood on the steps of my dorm. I was a step above him, at perfect kissing height. "Can I ask you a question?" I said.

"OK."

"Why haven't you kissed me?"

He furrowed his dark eyebrows. "I didn't think you wanted me to."

"Why not?"

"Because you never say you love me."

I stared at him and laughed. "Well how can I fall in love with you when you won't kiss me?"

He looked surprised and amused. Maybe he thought it was a shallow thing to say. But how could I tell him that he had a dead girl on his hands waiting to be resurrected? The daughter of Jairus (*She is not dead; she sleepeth*); Lazarus in the tomb, ready to be called to life. Come forth! I couldn't explain how cold, how lifeless I felt. I was floating apart from everything.

Probably he should have stuck to his guns: why should people play at love if they don't love each other? But the next night, out on the college baseball field again, Jon finally took me in his arms and kissed me. It was a kiss both warm and frightening: nothing like that earlier kiss on stage. We sat on extra coats on the snow, facing each other, cross-legged. He pulled me to him: I softened and melted against his chest. I slipped my hand around his back. His body was so different from my own: he was broad-shouldered and bony, with a rough face and thick skin across the back of his neck. The wind was cold and made my eyes tear up, but I really did want to cry. Now again more than ever I had that feeling of wanting to reel the whole world into my heart—to keep pulling and pulling until it was all gathered up inside of me. I felt affection welling up, not only for him, but for everything. I wanted to be connected to everyone.

Every night after that we went out and kissed each other for a long time. We kissed on the baseball field, under stairwells in my dorm, in the aisles of the college bookstore (he had a night janitorial job). All day in classes I thought about kissing him; I walked around smiling.

"If there's a heaven," I asked Pam, "do you know what I think it'll be like?"

"What?"

"In heaven we'll all be completely connected—no barriers anymore, no distance. We'll be like one person."

She gasped. "That sounds like hell!"

Through most of college, I'd had a job as a projectionist for the audio-visual services department. This involved dragging film projectors and other media paraphernalia all over campus, setting up the equipment, and being ready to repair it in the middle of a classroom emergency. I loved this job because I did most of my duties in the pitch dark. I could sleep through dull movies, like "Molecular Chain Reactions," but stay awake, if I chose, for the interesting ones, such as "Human Reproduction at a Glance." Often I studied by flashlight, stopping to look at those great wheels of film whirring above me, the cone of golden dust glimmering from the lens. The digital generation will never appreciate the more primitive miracle of the film projector.

Sometimes, now, Jon came along with me to show movies. One day we were showing a film version of James Joyce's *Ulysses* to an English class. The professor had already informed me in a firm tone that he hoped we wouldn't be having any of those "infernal technical difficulties which plague the audio-visual department." I assured him that things would be fine. I proceeded then to set up the projector, get it going, and sit down very close to Jon in the back of the room, watching intently and thinking we should have brought popcorn.

About twenty minutes later, Jon suddenly sat up and whispered, "Betty, look!" I turned to where he was pointing and jumped from my seat. The takeup reel was broken. About a mile of celluloid lay in a huge pile on the floor.

"Tell the professor you have to stop the movie," Jon whispered.

"I can't. He'll kill me."

I stood behind the camera and very carefully wound the back reel by hand at slightly accelerated speed, until it had caught up with the front. Then I kept standing there, standing all through the movie version of one of the longest books in the English language, turning the back reel with one finger. The professor and his class watched their movie, slept and daydreamed, never suspecting that such heroism was going on right in the same room. Jon whispered words of encouragement; eventually he even took over. As I watched the film move across the light, I thought what an interesting metaphor a projector made for love. It reminded me of some lines from a T.S. Eliot poem that I'd read in a seminar class:

At the still point of the turning world. Neither flesh nor fleshless;
Neither from nor towards; at the still point, there the dance is,
But neither arrest nor movement. And do not call it fixity,
Where past and future are gathered. Neither movement from
nor towards,
Neither ascent nor decline. Except for the point, the still point . . .

Desire itself is movement
Not in itself desirable;
Love is itself unmoving,
Only the cause and end of movement,
Timeless and undesiring . . .
Sudden in a shaft of sunlight
Even while the dust moves . . .*

The heart, open and loving, longs to reel the world into itself. Yes, the movement defines itself around particular loves: first the love of a child for the parent, later the desire of the lover for the beloved, even later the love of the parent for the child. Still, those strong desires are only the wheels that bear the whole world into the lover's heart. At the center of desire, both shining through and inhabiting all, is Love itself: the light of the world, the still point at the heart of everything, timeless and undesiring.

The metaphor was a sort of revelation to me, or perhaps the revelation gave me the metaphor. I saw what I had been seeking, both intellectually and emotionally. I'd felt isolated: I'd been looking for a connecting center, a relationship among all the estranged elements of the world. If Jesus Christ was really at the center of everything (as T.S. Eliot also thought), both holding it together and giving it purpose, then how could I ever feel alone again? I was connected to him and through him to everything else. Strangely enough, it was my love for one person that set this connection in motion. The more I began to love Jon, the more I felt my connection to God, and the more I longed to draw the whole world to him through myself.

My heart was open and happy.

12.

a pregnant metaphor

Whosoever drinketh of this water shall thirst again;
But whosoever drinketh of the water that I shall give him
shall never thirst,
but the water that I shall give him shall be in him
a well of water springing up into everlasting life.
—John 4:13–14

I had felt empty and famished. I'd hungered and thirsted for love, and thought that love would never come. How could I be worthy of it? How could anyone love me? My greatest loves in the past had taken place mainly in my own mind. They were secret, overwhelming obsessions that I'd had for people who often barely took notice of me. I'd felt chained to my own feelings, and I assumed I wouldn't know how to give free, generous affection even if someone asked for it; I certainly wouldn't know how to receive such love if someone offered it.

Then Jon came. After an initial struggle to love him, I thought *God is filling me up at last, giving me my heart's desire.* I saw this new love as a fountain to drink from, a source of limitless joy. Once I'd tasted the water, I couldn't seem to drink my fill of it. I wanted Jon with me all the time, never out of sight. I wanted to pull him down with me in love and never let him go.

I invited him home to Atlanta at the beginning of the summer: we rode a hot bus down from Chicago, and for the whole trip—twenty-one hours, including a breakdown on a country highway—I sat clinging to him, kissing him, coaching him shamelessly on what to say and not to say to make my family like him. He enjoyed the affection, of course, but he found it rather wild, too. Where had this strange girl come from? Were all women like this? After refusing to say "I love you" for months, after keeping such a critical distance, I was suddenly acting like Anna Karenina with Vronsky.

"I dream about you all the time," I wrote him that summer, when he'd taken the bus back to Wheaton alone. "I want to be with you. I want to be yours, forever."

We got engaged the following Christmas and planned to be married after I graduated. That spring, the student association announced an essay contest on "identifying and solving the problems of the world." The midsemester break was almost upon us; nearly everyone was packing for home or crash-studying for finals. I had lots of work, too, but a nameless donor had put up a three-thousand-dollar prize for the essay, and I could think of so many things to do with three thousand dollars, so many problems to solve, though they weren't actually the world's problems, only the problems of two people who were about to get married and needed some extra cash. Jon sat beside me all that week while I thwacked at the typewriter keys. At the end of the last paragraph, when I'd put the last period on the last sentence, I pushed the return key and the carriage flung hard to the right, knocking a cup of boiling hot tea over onto his foot.

So he entered married life with a slight limp and a wife who'd won three thousand dollars. We blew most of the money on a honeymoon to England. It was like something out of Dickens, this piece of good fortune from an anonymous benefactor. For the first day, I really thought England smelled better than America. I kept rolling down the windows of the rental car, taking deep breaths, and saying, "Wow! Everything must be blooming here! The air is so sweet!"

Finally Jon said, "Are you sure you're not smelling the air freshener in the glove compartment?" I checked and yes, I was. But that didn't make me cynical. Nothing could make me cynical about England: not the lack of sweet perfume in the air, nor the awful M roads, nor the drab suburbs around London, nor the owner of the bed-and-breakfast who tried to run over his wife with a Volkswagen on our first night together, near Stonehenge.

Rural England was the most beautiful place I'd ever seen. Its peaceful hills were so green, its villages and churches so lovely. The clear skies above us reflected our unbounded joy in each other. It seemed to me that God had answered my prayers once and for all, both for love and for faith. I looked around and saw England as I saw the rest of life ahead: the fulfillment of dreams.

How can anyone remember exactly when happiness ends and misery begins? To live in time is like walking along a measured field, passing from one point to the next. To remember time is like looking down into a lake. We don't see separate points in the water: the shallows reveal the depths but they also color and distort them, so that the close past and the deep past become an inseparable whole. I stand here in the present, looking down into time, unable to distinguish my recent feelings from what came long before, unable to say for sure what the truth is. I remember that our first year of marriage was happy. We lived in Wheaton, right across from train tracks. Trains rumbled back and forth and blew their horns, day and night, every fifteen minutes. For furniture we had an old green sofa, a lamp in the shape of an American eagle, my father's army trunk, and four metal folding chairs set around a formica-topped table. We stored our clothes in two matching cardboard boxes, set on their sides. We slept on a double bed under a quilt made by Jon's grandmother years before.

Jon worked for a Japanese printing company; I worked at the college. We had no real concern for our future, no plans to acquire good furniture, for instance, or a car without rust, or more money. We spent what money we did have on Chinese food and movies. In the winter we walked in the snow. In the spring we strolled up and down the prairie path for miles and played basketball at the court down the street.

I self-consciously took up righteous habits. I read my Bible regularly and prayed. I tutored a refugee, visited an elderly woman, taught a children's Pioneer Club. Such good works had always been advertised to me as the indispensable activities of any red-blooded evangelical woman: they were the things I'd been prepared to do since childhood, though I'd rarely done them and in some cases actually scorned the people who did. Now I'd put scorn behind me. Bring on Bible studies! Prayer meetings! Vacation Bible School! Potlucks! I couldn't get enough of love or righteousness.

We left Wheaton after a year, but I don't want to leave it so quickly, this time. I want to linger there a little longer, remembering. There were good friends around, and parties; winter walks with the world frozen white and the sky above me as blue as a swimming pool. There were red geraniums glowing in the windows of the Wade Center, where I worked; my friend Virginia and I pretending to be British schoolgirls, referring to each other as "old thing" and making fun of the more serious types. My boss, Lyle, popping in and out of the office, calling me "Frau Carter," talking endlessly about Airedales and offering us chocolates.

And then it was summer, intensely hot outside and dry. People were fretting about global warming, predicting that Chicago would be as hot as Memphis in a mere fifty years. Jon gave a lot of thought to the nearer future. He wanted to be a teacher, but he needed more education. So we decided to move back to Georgia for graduate school. We bought an old pickup. We said good-bye to our friends. We took our ugly furniture outside and set it by the dumpster behind the apartments. Then we packed up what was left and headed south, driving back roads all the way. It was a long trip, but we were both sick of suburban Chicago and wanted to see the real country. We took turns driving while the other one put bare feet up on the dashboard and hung an arm out the passenger window. If we'd had a dog, we'd have kept it up front between us, panting and chewing on the stick shift.

I didn't know it then, but I already feared the changes to come—a disconnection from Wheaton and the recent past. Experience had taught me that love itself was contextual, grounded in a place and time. Exile from a place could disrupt love and break connections that were invulnerable to every other force, even death and unfaithfulness. I wanted to assure myself that there would be no exile this time. Where we were going wasn't a new world, but a tangent to this one. If that was so, then a connecting point must exist between the two worlds, and I wanted to find it. What was the particular spot where the Midwest ended and the South began: the still point, that center that held the margins of existence in relation?

I watched the country fly by from the open window, and I tried to see the connection. Maybe the connection came where the prairie stopped and the land rippled out in undulating green; maybe it was the town of Madison, Indiana, where the road dipped down deep to the Ohio River before it sprang back up to Kentucky. I'm not at all sure that one connecting point existed, and if it did, I somehow missed it. I only know that once we finally crossed into North Georgia, we'd come to an utterly different world. This new world was my old one, the South. Yet it was so far from the place I'd recently come to love that I couldn't see it now as real.

I wanted to feel happy with the change. Jon was obviously happy. From the day we arrived in town, he went around liking everything: liking the streets, the restaurants, the university, the new apartment. I felt my old sense of exile rushing in, the despair of belonging nowhere and to no one; having no name or relation to the world. Emotionally, I simply couldn't handle the notion that a place (Wheaton) could still exist in my heart but not be present in time and space. What happened to the past when the people and places of the past were scattered? Did it still have meaning? Was it lost forever? I felt that I could start walking northwest and walk for the rest of my life, but I'd go around in circles, never to find that part of the world again.

This feeling was no surprise to me. I'd had it each time I moved, and I should have known by now that it would eventually go away: all sadness passes with time; all grief changes. In relation to Jon, though, it taught me something important. Love itself was no guarantee against homesickness. I'd thought that romantic love symbolized the incarnation in that it bound a human being to the world and infused everything with greater meaning. Now I wondered whether love had any lasting significance at all. Maybe it was an ephemeral feeling, passing quickly with changing places and times. I loved my husband—clung to him, actually, as one familiar thing in the shifting surface of the world—but I wasn't sure what it meant to love him here. I once again felt rootless and adrift.

Mama and Daddy now lived an hour away, in Chestnut Mountain, Georgia. They gave us a couch and a bookshelf, which we carried home to Athens in the pickup truck. Mama came to visit and asked where I was planning to serve my husband supper, since I didn't have a table.

"Well, we have a bar in the kitchen," I said, defensively.

"You're not going to eat at that *bar!*"

"You make it sound like I'll be serving gin and tonics. Who needs a table? We'll eat on the couch, in front of the TV."

Actually, I'd have liked a table, or a comfortable chair, or a pretty rug, or anything to give me some feeling of home.

This in itself was funny, because for the last year I'd been living happily with next to nothing, surviving out of a box. Now, apparently, I needed more.

"What's home to you?" I asked Jon one evening. "Does Japan still feel like home to you?"

"Home is where you are," he said, and I felt a stab of shame. I wanted to say the same thing, but I didn't feel it.

"Don't you miss Japan?" I asked him.

"Yes. But it's been so long since I lived there."

"What about Wheaton? Do you miss it?"

"Sure." He smiled. "But I'm used to missing places. Betty, do you know where home is to you?"

"No."

"Home to you is always the place you've just left."

I laughed. I knew he was probably right, since a few years before, as a college freshman, I'd resented Wheaton and missed my old friends in Georgia. Now I resented Georgia and felt homesick for Wheaton. Was it that my heart held on stubbornly to whatever was tugged away from me, pulled out of my reach? It seemed that whatever I couldn't have became the thing that mattered most. I didn't want to be that way: I wanted to be settled here and content with a husband who loved me. But I didn't know how to change something so fundamental about myself as discontent.

That first year in Athens crawled by. Our truck quit working almost immediately, so we went nearly everywhere on foot or by bus. We found a good church and made new friends, but I continued to miss the old ones. Needing money, we decided I should take the first job I was offered—a menial position in the book-ordering section of the main library. It required a great tolerance of monotony and a superhuman attention to detail. Now when I typed words on the wrong keys (titles of books, mainly, including *Hpmr eoyj yjr Eomf*—a Georgia classic), I caught the wrath of the supervisor, who called me "baby doll" and "sweetheart" and then demanded to know how I could be so f—— stupid. I missed my old job, with the Airedales and chocolates.

If I had only been unhappy about the change of circumstances, I guess my unhappiness would have eased as our circumstances settled. But a slippage of faith apparently accompanied my slip from joy. I felt a dull, persistent doubt, a spiritual emptiness that I knew was related to the recent exile, but also to some more profound loss—some deep wound that the move had opened up again.

One day, I cursed. I don't remember whether I actually said anything aloud: the curse was against the Holy Spirit, and the words seemed to have a will of their own. I pushed them away, but they came back. They jumped into my thoughts and I pushed them away again, harder, but they sprang back again and sent me into paroxysms of guilt. The harder I tried not to say or think the words, the more I wanted to think and say them.

I found a manual of psychiatry at the library that told me I was experiencing compulsive episodes not uncommon among religious subjects: the persistent, uncontrollable recurrence of blasphemous thoughts. Some unfortunate people, apparently, actually stood up and shouted blasphemy in the middle of sermons.

I never cursed the Holy Spirit out loud in church, but I cursed him in my head. Curses came to me when I was praying, when I was singing, when I was thinking, reading, writing. . . . Each time I recoiled in horror, then cursed God again and asked forgiveness, then cursed God again and asked forgiveness again, and so on. The struggle had a comic element: sometimes after cursing, I slapped myself across the cheek like a shocked Victorian maiden. I might have laughed, if I hadn't felt such guilt: I went to the Bible and looked up some verses about blasphemy against the Spirit.

All manner of sin and blasphemy shall be forgiven unto men; but the blasphemy against the Holy Ghost shall not be forgiven unto men. And whosoever speaketh a word against the Son of man, it shall be forgiven him; but whosoever speaketh against the Holy Ghost, it shall not be forgiven him, neither in this world, neither in the world to come.*

I remembered that when we were children we had asked our teachers what those verses meant—if we'd really go to hell for speaking against the Holy Spirit. Our teachers must have been ready for the question, because without hesitation they all said that, really, the unpardonable sin against the Holy Spirit was to reject God. Now I wondered if they had been saying that as a tricky way to get around an apparent contradiction in Presbyterian teaching: the fact that we were told we couldn't possibly lose our salvation, while here was biblical evidence that there was at least one sin too grave to be forgiven.

As soon as I'd begun believing in God again, I'd instinctively seen him through the lens of the gospel I'd heard all my life. Jesus had washed away our sins, removed our guilt, and brought us close to his Father. Even now I imagined God as loving and forgiving, yet I also saw him drifting further and further into the distance. I knew that this was an illusion: I was the one drifting, propelled by the fluttering and thrashing of my own shame. Still, I moved further out, imagining God spread behind me like a long white beach while I moved further to sea, unable to stop myself. I pictured the bond between us—the tether, the great umbilical chord—torn loose.

"Please have patience with me, God," I prayed. "Please don't let me go."

If I'd been an alcoholic, I might have taken up drinking again, to silence my brain, perhaps, and ease some of the guilt. But I was only a compulsive worshiper: I had one crying need that shouted down all others. It silenced hunger, thirst, curiosity, sexual desire, craving for beauty. No simple physical or intellectual desire could stand up to this emotional one—and that was to become drunk on another soul, on the very being of someone outside myself. I longed to draw someone in and feel that I wasn't alone.

The woman I attached myself to this time was needy in all senses of the word. I'd met her as soon as we arrived in town, and I started out with knee-jerk evangelical intentions of helping her. I lent her money and listened to her troubles. She'd told me she didn't believe in God, so I prayed sincerely that I might "minister" to her, "be a good witness," "show her Christian love." Pretty soon, though, I'd stepped back on the same old path I'd been traveling most of my life: obsession (wanting to know all about a person, wanting to be the most important person in her life), worry (being terrified that she'd find another friend and drop me), compulsion (driving past her house to see if she was home, calling her in order to hear her voice and then hanging up), and above all, *guilt guilt guilt* and more *guilt*. Also self-hatred over such out-of-balance love for her.

I could have lifted a page about the preacher's wife from my junior high diary and used it to describe my current obsession with this woman. The difference, though, was that my mother was no longer around to question my feelings:

the only one watching was my husband of two years. He appeared not to notice the stranger aspects of my behavior. At home he read his textbooks and wrote his papers. He met me at my lunch hour and discussed postmodernism with me over sandwiches. He railed against the evils of reader-response theory and cultural relativism. We talked about my job and our church and our new friends.

But Jon never asked me why I disappeared without explanation sometimes, why I cried for no reason, why I talked on the phone behind closed doors. I watched him with awe, admiring his apparent obliviousness, thinking that he was more like my father than I'd realized. How could he concentrate so well—put deep needs and longings aside (apart from sex) and focus on *things,* meaning any matter of interest from Georgia football to the work of some obscure German philosopher? It never occurred to me that Jon's obliviousness might be willful: that he might be afraid to look too hard at the woman he'd married.

He told me that once he was finished with school, I could take my turn and go back for a master's degree.

"That'll be great," I said happily, but I immediately seized up with fear. If I no longer spent my days on north campus, I wouldn't see my friend at all. The idea of separation made me panic. I'd have to arrange my life so that separation never happened. But how would I explain this to Jon? Here they came now, the troop of lies, marching to my

side: all my energies turned to protecting that one, invio-
lable friendship.

Did Jon know that I was suffering during this time? Yes,
of course he knew, but he shrank back. As for me, I wanted
him to rescue me, but I was afraid to ask him for it. I knew
what rescue would mean. It would mean having my obsessive
love torn away, a tearing that would mean pain for my husband
and me both. Our love would be tested. "Will you still love
me if I ask you to give this person up?" he would ask (maybe
not in those words, but I would understand the question).
And I would ask, "Can you be more to me than other men
have been? Can you come close, not just physically and
intellectually, but emotionally? Can you give me what I'm
looking for?"

I don't know how we would have answered, since neither
of us did ask. We conspired together not to disturb the calm
surface of our marriage. Neither of us made a move toward
the other, and, though we got along well, both of us felt
alone. One day at home I sat in a hot bath. Jon was in the
other room studying. Between us stood a thick, locked door.
I started weeping quietly, burying my face in a washcloth,
trying not to let him hear me. Yes, I wanted to share my
troubles with him. I also wanted to keep him at a distance. I
wanted him to burst through the door, to see me exposed.
But I was afraid. Fear told me to leave him be: let him to stay
in the other room with his books and be at peace.

And where was God then? Why didn't he come to me right away when I needed him, end the blasphemy in my head, end the obsession that humiliated me again and again? When I was a prisoner of my own thoughts, why didn't he come and cleanse my mind and give me relief?

Even as I say these things, I remember that I had good days in Athens. God must have been there glimmering through the everyday and the ordinary: speaking to me in kind words from friends, the beauty of north campus in the spring, Sunday dinners after church with our small congregation. When I visited the college Catholic center and watched the celebration of the Eucharist, I felt a desire for God that Presbyterian worship rarely provoked in me. It had to do with the Catholic view of Christ's presence in the elements of Communion. I wanted to believe that Christ really met human beings in a physical way, even now—I wanted the faith to accept that I could taste Christ in bread and wine. But I didn't have the faith. I thought Catholic doctrine was probably another beautiful dream.

In the fall, when Jon had started teaching, I found out I was pregnant. I was terrified. I doubted I'd make a good mother, since standards were apparently high: most of the people I knew complained about their parents. My sister gave me a book about pregnancy and child rearing, and I read it backward and forward, feeling more anxious every time I came to the page that reported "the daily routine of an actual new mother." The poor woman in the article was up and down all night, breastfeeding constantly, walking the crying baby around for hours in the afternoon, barely having time for a shower and never getting away for more than two hours at a time.

Meanwhile I was sicker than I'd ever been in my life. One day in December, I had to see the doctor for my regular checkup. I walked a mile and a half to Milledge Avenue, crossed the street at Five Points, and went another block to the old house where he had his office. I felt so weak: I'd been throwing up every day for almost three months now.

"You're far enough along for us to listen to the baby's heartbeat," he said.

"Oh, really?" I said, interested, but not thrilled. He laid the cold stethoscope on my lower abdomen, moving it around. On the ceiling above the examination table, someone had taped a poster of a Renaissance Madonna and Child. I looked at the pair curiously, wondering who around here cared about *art*. Surely not the doctor. He seemed like the kind who'd decorate his waiting room with framed posters from K-Mart. Suddenly we heard a rhythmic swoosh, swoosh, swoosh.

"Is that it?" I asked.

"That's it." he said. "There it is."

"It's so fast—" I couldn't help laughing. "Can I hear it again?"

"In a minute." He was ready to get on with the hateful part of the examination. He stretched and measured and probed, then told me I was doing fine and that he'd see me again in a month.

"Can I hear that heartbeat again?" I said.

"What? Oh, that's fine."

He laid his stethoscope on my stomach. There it was again. That swoosh, swoosh, swoosh.

"How come it beats so fast?" I said.

"Babies' hearts are like that."

"Oh."

He put away his instruments and left. I dressed and paid my bill, then went slowly out the front door and began to walk home. I talked to the baby as I walked. "I'm glad you're here. I'm going to take good care of you."

Over the next few weeks, I felt my obsession weakening, losing its hold on me, finally disappearing altogether. No single event had ever freed me so quickly and painlessly from an addiction to another person. For a little while I thought, "The miracle cure! Pregnancy! A baby! Why didn't I try this before?" I stopped cursing God, too, and began to think of myself as a fairly normal, well-balanced woman, who had only needed a healthy outlet for her time and energy. Now I focused on doing my best imitation of my own mother, transforming myself into a rational, dependable creature who could be trusted with the rearing of a small child. I read over the routine of that actual new mother again and began to prepare myself, buying cloth diapers and onesies and doing a painting for the baby's room.

Some people find themselves worshiping their children—even small children, or those not yet born. Babies are fragile and mysterious. In a metaphorical way they incarnate our hopes and expectations. We expect them to save us from disappointment and bring us happiness: what is a child if not desire made flesh?

But a baby is no savior and certainly no god. She is only a sacramental taste of God's grace: a sign of a sign, sent (in part) to embody a truth—that the world is empty and cries out to be filled with the divine: we are all empty and long to be filled with God.

Around Christmas, Jon and I went to a choir performance where a woman sang "Ave Maria." My brain had cleared, my thoughts (for a little while) were pure. I felt the baby move inside me, and for the first time I imagined how Mary must have felt. I'd never sympathized with her as I did now. What did she think as she laid her hand over her womb and felt the baby stretch and kick against her palm? It must have overwhelmed her to imagine that God lived under her heart. Not a *sign* of God, but *God*. God as a child, blessing her by drawing forth the one thing I'd never have thought God would need from us: our tenderness.

So many times I've questioned myself, wondered why even motherhood turned out not to be the satisfaction and end of all desires. But as surely as my mother and father had brought me God's grace with their protecting love, as surely as Jon had brought it to me with romantic love, that child growing in me brought a measure of God's grace by simply existing.

13

resting state

Now Thou art lifted up, draw me to Thee,
And at Thy death giving such liberal dole,
Moist with one drop of Thy blood, my dry soul.
                    —John Donne, "Crucifying"

We are all rather blessed in our deprivations if we let
ourselves be.
                    —Flannery O'Connor, *The Habit of Being*

The quiet of a new baby is deeper than most other human silence. Not one word scratches itself across the tablet of her thoughts. She drinks in the surface of the world by instinct, blinking her eyes at its brightness, plumbing its depths with unknown parts of herself. Suddenly the surface of the world changes: she opens her mouth and a cry escapes her lips. She doesn't know that she has cried out—doesn't even know that she is a presence or that another presence exists. Soon, though, she feels covered by enfolding warmth. She hears a familiar sound and turns her head, listening in utter silence.

On the night after my first daughter was born, she wailed for hours. I hadn't learned to nurse her yet, and I wasn't allowed to get out of bed to walk with her or rock her. All I could do was hold her tight against my neck and talk to her, as I'd done that day on our walk home from the doctor and so many days since. What to say, though? I was too tired to think of anything creative, so I said the first thing that came to mind, which was the Pledge of Allegiance:

I pledge allegiance to the flag of the United States of America, and to the Republic, for which it stands . . .

All at once, she stopped crying. Her head shifted toward me; her eyes searched the half-darkness. I quit reciting to listen to her silence. After a second, though, she let out another wail, so I started making noise again. This time I sang the French National Anthem:

Allons enfants de la patrie, le jour de gloire est arrive!

Once again, she quieted. It didn't matter what I said or in what language I said it. I kept talking and singing, running through my sketchy repertoire: the second chapter of Luke, the prologue to the *Aeneid*, an Italian proverb about cheese. I could have recited anything and she'd have listened. It was my voice that comforted her. My presence was enough. Soon her eyes fluttered closed and she slept until morning.

I've decided it's this kind of presence we all want, though we don't know we want it. We don't even have the language for it. Counselors talk about self-esteem, self-confidence, self-realization, empowerment, centering. To use such terms implies that we should be able to manage alone in the universe, given a happy childhood or at least very good therapy. While dependence is necessary for the very young, independence is the resting state of the full-grown human. Separation does bring natural sorrow for a time, but sorrow eases as the wounds of dependence close. After heartbreak or death, the self reconstructs its independent world.

What few of us want to imagine is that dependence may be our resting state: sorrow will always be with us. Blessed are those who mourn. We who were loved, who loved our mothers and fathers in return, grieve not over what we *didn't* have, but what we *had* and lost. We feel the distance of loss pushing into our hearts day by day, year by year, and know we can never go back to what has been.

By the time our second daughter was born, Jon and I had moved to a small town in Alabama. The wheel had turned again, for me: I was suffering another bad bout of obsession and depression. The person I loved this time didn't have any desire to be worshiped. We had one argument after another, and each time we argued, I went away despairing, feeling abandoned, sometimes suicidal.

"You know how you think you're going crazy?" my husband said one day after I'd had several sobbing fits. I stood with a towel wrapped around me and my hair wet, having just stepped out of the shower for the third time.

I nodded.

"Well, you're right," he said. "You are going crazy."

I started to cry. There was no more pretending. I could see that he was frightened and even angry.

"I'm sorry," he said. "I don't want to hurt you."

I couldn't keep from shaking. "I'm sorry, too. I can't seem to get control of myself. What should I do?"

"I have no idea how to help you."

I couldn't think of anything else to say. I went back to our bedroom and closed the door and cried some more, praying, "Why, God, *why*? Please take this agony away from me."

One morning I sat in a church Bible study, holding my baby daughter on my lap. Several women sat around me, all young mothers, gentle and devout, the kind of sweet Christian daughters my mother should have had if life made any sense. An older woman was teaching up front but I wasn't listening. I no longer listened to lessons or sermons, ever. A waste of time. So many words and never any satisfaction or relief from pain. I spent time with church people now only to avoid being alone.

At the moment, among these women, I'd lost all sense of time. Time didn't matter anyway. Time was a series of movements from one place to the next, one duty to the next, all eventually swallowed up in the greater movement of humanity toward no place in particular. I'd reached the place I'd feared so much as a child: sadness and hopelessness and endless boredom. This was my seat in the window, where I stared out at the world, waiting for the next world to take me away. I wondered what the gentle, devout church women would think of me if they actually saw *me*, as I was. Then a question came into my mind:

"*What do you want? What do you really want?*"

When you're addicted to another person, your first instinct is to answer that question with a name. "I want ___. Then I'd be happy." As a child I would have answered quickly with one name or another: "I want my mother," or my Sunday school teacher, or the woman I gave the baby shower for, or my karate teacher, or the preacher's wife. . . . But so many names later, with many loves come and gone, I was skeptical of my own desires. I wanted the love of one particular friend intensely, but I knew that this wanting would pass and there would be other wantings, other agonies ahead. I thought shamefully of a string of names, twenty or more people I'd once loved with all my heart, felt sure I couldn't live without. Now the idea of them didn't move me at all, didn't make my heart leap with joy or bring tears to my eyes. What I wanted was someone or something that had no name: it was unknown and unknowable.

I understood it best when I looked down at the baby on my lap. Having nursed, she slept quietly. When she woke up, she'd cry and I'd comfort her and maybe nurse her again. Her entire life was a melodrama of longings and satisfactions. Her expectation of love was as raw and new as she was. The more sure she felt that comfort was on its way, the louder and more insistently she cried for it. "I long for you!" her cry said. "Why are you taking so long?"

"You..."

My longing was the same as hers, only without the raw hope of satisfaction. I'd spent most of the last twenty years wrestling my desires, throttling them to the ground. What would happen if I let them go? Where would they take me? To what disappointments, to what destruction?

The love I wanted was mother love: energetic and sacrificial, all-seeing and all-rescuing. This was the love I pled for, cried for, bargained for, and schemed for from people who couldn't give it, no matter how hard I worked or what I sacrificed. In my rational moments I knew that it was wrong, even freakish, for a grown woman to long for a mother. I was, after all, a mother myself. I had two small children who depended on me to be energetic and sacrificial, all-seeing and all-rescuing.

But I had no control over this strange hunger. I could hide it for a while until the compulsiveness returned, and then you'd see me circling one house, dialing one number, waiting for one call. On a warm April morning, having just dropped off my children at school, I saw that woman I currently loved most, *worthy object of all affection and adoration,* drive out of the parking lot with another friend. She had told me she was too busy to have coffee that day. I sped back home and dialed her number again and again. Hours went by. She must still be out with the *other woman.* At 2:30 I got my kids from school and went straight back home to the phone and dialed once more.

"Hello?" she finally said.

I burst into tears. "Why did you have to go out with *her?* You left school right in front of me. You knew I'd see you."

She took a deep breath, obviously measuring out her words. "Do you think we're joined at the hip, Betty?"

"No, but you lied to me."

"Listen to me," she said in a determined voice, "because I'm going to tell you something. Are you listening?"

"Yes."

"I know you struggle, and I feel for you. But sometimes you act like a *stalker.* And that scares me. You act like one of those people who *stalks* people."

I put my hand over the mouthpiece of the phone.

"Are you there?" she said.

"Stalker." I drew out the word in a whisper, examining it. "Are you all right?"

I stared at the ceiling and said it again, more boldly. "*Stalker.*"

"Listen," she said a second time, and again I listened. She backpedaled, trying to soften what she'd already said. But the strange thing was that I didn't want her to un-say it, as painful as it was to hear. When you've become so difficult that the person you want most in the world fears you, when many people only love you out of mercy or pity, and even lie to keep you calm or keep you at bay, then one cruel but honest word sounds like a message straight from God. There's salvation in that single true word; you feel like Elijah being fed by the sharp beaks of ravens.

"Are you there?" she said. "I didn't want to hurt you."

"No, you're right," I said. "You're absolutely right about me. I better not call you for a while."

And I put down the phone.

It was as if I walked again in a dark hall as a child and I heard the strange voice call me. But this time I didn't allow myself to yell for my mother. I waited to see what the thing was that had my name on the tip of its tongue. I waited in the dark, sweating with fear, until the voice called out:

"Betty," it said. "Betty."

I didn't run. I let it come closer, so that I could almost feel it breathing over the back of my neck. I turned, expecting a monster. But what I saw was much worse. It was *nothingness*. Nothingness and isolation, separation and death. The door stood open at the end of the hall and the light was off and there was now no one lying in my mother and father's bed. I was all alone.

One morning a few months later, I sat at home, trying to write but unable to. It was a sunny day in late September. A warm breeze blew in the open window over my desk, stirring the red petals of a geranium, stirring the leaves of blank yellow paper under my hand. I felt as if I'd been crying for weeks straight, but now more tears came. Why is it that beauty stirs desire? Stirs it, but doesn't satisfy it. A changing wind, the smell of grass and dry leaves: these are sacraments of memory. They bring the past directly to our senses: we remember similar beauties from long ago, in other summers ending, other autumns beginning. Memory rising in us stirs up desire, not just for glimpses and visions, signs and symbols, but for someone who is now no longer there.

I remembered an older, unmarried woman who'd told me that she opened up her hope chest one day and pulled out the lingerie her mother had set aside for her years before. All those beautiful gowns were moth-eaten and decayed: they fell apart in her hands. This was how love looked to me now. Wasted. Turned to threads.

I left the window and got in bed and lay curled up on my side, staring at the dust as it struggled to rise in a stream of sunlight. I was going to a counselor once a week, and taking an antidepressant. These things had helped me see myself more clearly; they'd also brought me a measure of self-control. But they hadn't brought me closer to what I wanted. I had made a resolution not to let myself call any friends for comfort (detox), yet I couldn't help wishing somebody might call me. Not a rescuing hero, not the savior of my soul. Just a telemarketer. Someone to say, "How are you today?" Sympathy might not heal me, but I'd be glad for it. Couldn't someone for once *come to me, search me out* without being asked?

Apparently not. That was too much to expect from God or the universe.

A picture fluttered through my mind of myself on a really bad day, years before: I'd been out of control; I'd written a secret letter to someone's old high school in Wisconsin, pretending to be a former classmate and asking for a yearbook photo. Now I shuddered with disgust at the thought. I said, "You don't deserve love after some of the things you've done."

I met my own eyes in the mirror across the room. "None of those people you worshiped ever really loved you. You wanted them to, but how could they? You've been a trial to your family and your friends. You've sucked away at everyone, trying to be happy. And now you're wishing somebody would love you, but the fact is that you're not lovable."

The words were bitter. "You're not *lovable,*" I said. "In fact, you're not even *loving.* Your love—everybody's love—is fragile and selfish and conditional. We think we love people, but we only use them."

The breeze had stilled outside; the house was so quiet that I could hear the cat snoring down the hall. I cleared my mind and stared at the mirror, waiting.

And then something changed. It was as if a clock had stopped, and now started moving in reverse. I felt a sense of unwinding. The present uncoiled like a long, long thread into the past. The hopes and shames of recent years slipped further away from me—all of my loves, my disappointments growing smaller, until at last I lay with nothing in my heart but an unnamed desire. I said a prayer that would have curled my mother's hair.

I don't love you, Jesus. I'm sorry, but I just don't love you. Half the time I don't even believe in you. But you're the only one who loves me, so please help me love you. And please love me. Please love me.

These words had been given to me, but I said them from my heart. They were both the truest expression of my weakness and the fullest unfolding yet of the faith planted in me so many years before.

For most of my life the gospel had hung in the air like rain that wouldn't fall. Dark, heavy rain. I'd tasted it in the wind, I'd breathed it, cursed it. Now it came rushing down.

Here was the thing I'd walked the aisle so many times as a child to find, putting one small foot in front of the other, all the way to the cross and the old Remembrance table, keeping my eyes on my mother up in the choir loft, walking toward my father, who both mirrored God and blocked my view of him. "Come to the cross," Daddy had said, gripping his Bible, and we'd all sung, *Amazing grace, how sweet the sound that saved a wretch like me! I once was lost, but now am found, was blind but now I see.* I hadn't believed then that I was lost, or that God searched for me or wanted to bring me home. I'd assumed that "home" was right there at the front of the church, and I'd wondered why, the harder I tried to step toward it, the further away it moved.

But for all those years, that cross had sat at the front of our bright church, often hidden among gladiolas and ferns, occasionally set aside to make room for offering plates or the elements of Communion. Quietly, patiently it had reminded us of the man who waited for us at the end of the aisle. He waited for me now. He longed for me, pursued me with visions, hunted me with dreams.

I am your father and mother, lover and friend, the *Why,* the *You.*

This Do in Remembrance of Me.

Walking his red-washed aisle as a child, I hadn't known that the aisle itself was a symbol of the sorrowful path I would walk later; that it was a symbol of Calvary, the way of suffering, where Jesus was stretched out and lifted up, alone. He became our bloody bridge from earth to heaven, from the wilderness of exile to our temple, our Jerusalem. Now, when at last I stepped into his path, I found that he shared my sorrows:

> *O strong Ram, which hast battered heaven for me,*
> *Mild Lamb, which with Thy blood hast marked*
> *the path;*
> *Bright Torch, which shin'st, that I the way may see . . .***

For the next two hours I slept and prayed, slept and prayed. I didn't pray for friendship, beauty, affection, or even goodness. Those desires would be back. They were already clamoring at the door. For now, I only wanted Jesus.

notes

Introduction

*John Donne, "Sonnet 10," of *Holy Sonnets*.

**Mark 15:34.

Chapter 2

*George Bennard, "The Old Rugged Cross" (Chicago: Word, Inc., The Rodeheaver Co., 1913, 1941), all rights reserved.

**Ralph E. Hudson, Refrain, in "At the Cross," by Isaac Watts.

***Charles Wesley, "And Can It Be."

****Mark 14:34.

*****Mark 15:34. Jesus was quoting from Psalm 22: "My God, my God, why hast thou forsaken me? why art thou so far from helping me, and from the words of my roaring? O my God, I cry in the daytime, but thou hearest not; and in the night season, and am not silent."

Chapter 3

*Matthew 10:39b.

**"I Wish We'd All Been Ready," words and music by Larry Norman, Beechwood Music Corp. and J.C. Love Publishing Co., 1969.

Chapter 4

Epigraph. From "American Karate," a manual for the purple belt program.

* Luke 2:49.

**Matthew 5:11–12.

***Helen H. Lemmel, "Turn Your Eyes Upon Jesus" (1922, 1950).

Chapter 5

*Genesis 32:24–32.

Chapter 6

*Luke 17:21.

**John 4:23.

***Joachim Neander, "Praise to the Lord, the Almighty," translated by Catherine Winkworth.

Chapter 7

Epigraph. Edgar Allan Poe, "The Premature Burial," in *Edgar Allan Poe Stories: Twenty-Seven Thrilling Tales by the Master of Suspense, Edgar Allan Poe* (New York: Platt & Munk, 1961), pp. 379–380.

*Poe, "The Telltale Heart," p. 17.

**"The Telltale Heart," p. 17.

Chapter 8

*Ezekiel 1:4, 26.

**John Milton, from "L'Allegro."

***Alfred Lord Tennyson, from *The Princess.*

****Psalm 19:1–3.

Chapter 10

*Gary Chapman, "Father's Eyes" (Paragon Music Corporation, 1978).

** *The Confessions of St. Augustine*, translated by Rex Warner (New York: Mentor Book, New American Library, 1963), p. 17.

*** *The Confessions*, p. 52.

****It's probably important to note that Augustine distrusted physical desire, believing (perhaps from dualistic reflexes) that sexual longing muddied the waters of spiritual love.

Chapter 11

*Matthew 11:28.

**T. S. Eliot, from "Burnt Norton," *The Complete Poems and Plays, 1909–1950* (San Diego: Harcourt Brace Jovanovich Publishers, 1971).

Chapter 12

*Matthew 12:31–32.

Chapter 13

* John Newton, "Amazing Grace."

**John Donne, from "Ascension" (7 in *La Corona*).

Acknowledgments

Thanks to Jon, Joanna, and Emma for their love and patience. Thank you to all family and friends—especially Gordon Bals, for his wisdom, and Burt and Anita Boykin for their faithfulness. Finally, many thanks to Lil Copan, who drew this out of me and then worked hard to make it better.